Celebrating the Disciplines

Celebrating
the Disciplines

A Journal Workbook to Accompany

Celebration of Discipline

Richard J. Foster &
Kathryn A. Helmers

HarperOne
An Imprint of HarperCollins*Publishers*

HarperOne

CELEBRATING THE DISCIPLINES: *A Journal Workbook to
Accompany* Celebration of Discipline. Copyright © 1992 by
HarperCollins Publishers. All rights reserved.
Printed in the United States of America. No part of this
book may be used or reproduced in any manner whatsoever
without written permission except in the case of brief
quotations embodied in critical articles and reviews. For
information address HarperCollins Publishers,
10 East 53rd Street, New York, NY 10022.

HarperCollins books may be purchased for educational,
business, or sales promotional use. For information please write:
Special Markets Department, HarperCollins Publishers,
10 East 53rd Street, New York, NY 10022.

HarperCollins Web site: http://www.harpercollins.com

HarperCollins®, ⚒®, and HarperOne™ are trademarks of
HarperCollins Publishers.

LC: 88–45135

ISBN: 978–0–06–069867–6

07 08 09 10 11 HAD 40 39 38 37 36 35 34 33 32 31

Contents

An Invitation

I invite you to the double search: we who are searching for God, and God who is searching for us. The first, of course, could not happen without the second. God is the initiator. It is he who plants the yearning in our heart for him in the first place. "Our heart is restless until it finds rest in Thee," said Saint Augustine. Surely we love him only because he first loved us—loved us with an overpowering, unreasonable, outrageous kind of love.

This great and glorious truth does not, however, make our searching any less real or any less important. God invites us to seek him, and to seek him with all our heart. And the wonder is this: the finding intensifies the seeking all the more. One taste of the heavenly manna and all other pursuits pale by comparison. We want more: more love, more freedom, more of God in our lives.

Down through the centuries of Christian faith and practice we are told that our side of the pursuit of God is discovered in the classic disciplines of the spiritual life. "The means of grace," they have been sometimes called. Things like prayer and solitude and simplicity and service. These activities of body, mind, and spirit are the means God uses for bringing us into growing conformity to Jesus Christ. They are how we follow him in continuing discipleship—what we could call "the path of disciplined grace."

Welcome, then, to this wonderful search—wonderful because no matter how much we may pursue God we always discover that The Seeking God has been pursuing us all the more.

Richard Foster

Introduction:
Journey Through the Disciplines

"We need not be well advanced in matters of theology to practice the Disciplines," writes Richard Foster. "The primary requirement is a longing after God." The intent of this workbook is to assist you in developing that longing through cultivating life in the Spirit.

Celebration of Discipline charts the path to spiritual growth through the classical Disciplines of Christian devotion and practice. This workbook has been created to augment Richard Foster's book by providing a guide for exploring these Disciplines, using *Celebration of Discipline* as the primary reference.

Although this companion guide is designed to provide a structure with enough direction to help individuals and groups stay on track over a twelve-month period, you need not commit to a whole year in order to benefit from exploring the Disciplines. This workbook is arranged in four parts that build on each other but are flexible enough to stand alone. Each part corresponds to one quarter of a year, and within each quarter there are separate sections on each Discipline. This organization opens up various ways to approach the journey through the Disciplines. For example, you might choose any of the following strategies:

- Proceed through one quarter at a time, with breaks in between, continuing with as many of the four as your time and interest permit.
- Dip in and out of the material on the various Disciplines without following the suggested structure, working on those areas in which you feel a special need or desire for further growth.
- Embark on the year-long structure, making the commitment as an individual or in a group, and build in time for breaks between weeks or quarters. You may find that stepping back from your journey periodically will refresh your perspective and enthusiasm.

Throughout this flexible structure, there are further opportunities for personalizing the journey built into the suggestions offered. Although we are called to practice the Spiritual Disciplines, we are not all called to practice them in just the same way. Feel free to adapt your journey to your own needs and sense of calling.

FORMAT

The journey through the Disciplines presented in this workbook is fundamentally structured around the four quarters (thirteen weeks) of a twelve-month period.

The first quarter encompasses an overview of the Disciplines. Weekly segments will lead you through *Celebration of Discipline* one chapter at a time, with questions for reflection on the reading and on Scripture. These weekly segments also contain suggestions for experimental practice of the Disciplines and for reflecting on the journey in journal form.

After this initial overview period, the guide changes rhythm for a more in-depth exploration. The second, third, and fourth quarters open up the Inward, Outward, and Corporate Disciplines respectively. Starting each quarter is a "hinge week" for celebration, reflection, and planning, which will prompt you to look back as well as ahead for personalizing the next segment of your journey through the respective four Disciplines.

Although you will find space throughout this workbook for recording notes and reflections, you may benefit most by keeping a separate journal. A simple spiral-bound notebook is all you need, if you do not already maintain a personal journal. Using a separate journal will enhance the value of this guide by giving you a place to draw back from the "do-list" feel of the many suggestions for practice. It will also prove an invaluable tool as both a planning guide and a place set apart for reflection.

A special section in the back of this workbook, "Record of Commitments" (see page 203), supplements the main content by providing one place where you can keep track of major intentions or goals for practice. If you review it and update it periodically, you will not only have a handy and accessible reference but also a way to check yourself against overly ambitious planning. Maintaining a clear, straight-forward perspective overall will help keep you from feeling overwhelmed or confused.

After the four quarters, the overall journey is brought to a point of resolution with a closing retreat. Here individuals and groups have the opportunity to set apart two days for reflecting on their journey through the Disciplines and evaluating how to carry forward its impact in healthy patterns of long-term practice.

A NOTE ABOUT INDIVIDUAL AND GROUP USE

The contents of this guide have been created for both individual and group use.

Throughout the guide, individuals are encouraged to avoid isolation and share their journey with others. This can be done in several ways. One option is to seek the guidance of a spiritual companion or mentor for the duration of the journey. Another option is to take advantage of the opportunities suggested throughout this guide for linking up with others. Still another way to share the journey is to pull together an informal group for a specific purpose on selected occasions.

There are many explicit suggestions for group activities embedded in the ideas for practicing the Disciplines. These ideas would work well for loosely gathered groups of individuals who desire to meet periodically to share their respective journeys, practice some of the Disciplines in community, or simply encourage each other along the way.

Those who are using this workbook as part of a group commitment will discover a wealth of opportunities for group exploration and interaction among Christians within all traditions and denominations. Groups may opt to commit to one quarter at a time with breaks in between, or they might decide to choose the full year, allowing an additional couple of months to accommodate breaks, special observances of holy days and seasons, and adjustments to synchronize individual schedules.

The frequency of group meetings can be varied according to group needs and desires. Weekly meetings could coincide with the suggested time frame of this guide, which divides up the twelve months of the journey into fifty-two weeks as the basic units of structure. If the group prefers, biweekly or monthly meetings would also work well as times in which participants can encourage each other as they share their significant experiences and major insights or struggles. Especially during emphasis on the Corporate Disciplines, but also during the earlier quarters, there are many opportunities for planning specific group activities centered around communal practice of the Disciplines.

Because of the variety of options in this workbook emphasizing personal choice and flexibility, it is not necessary to appoint one group leader to guide participants through the process or through individual meetings. Instead, the group may want to rotate leadership in particular aspects of their interaction, such as praying, worshiping, sharing experiences, discussing issues, making group decisions, opening and closing group meetings, and planning special events or activities.

To achieve a healthy cross-section of individuals, facilitate easy interaction, and foster spiritual intimacy, it may be best to target three to seven people for the number of participants in a given group. Each person should have a copy of the workbook as well as a copy of *Celebration of Discipline* (preferably the revised edition introduced in 1988). It would also be helpful to ensure group access to reference materials on Bible study and the Christian tradition.

The closing retreat provides an ideal way for groups to celebrate their year together.

OPENING THE DOOR TO SPIRITUAL GROWTH

The Disciplines are presented here as the doorway to spiritual growth, not as a course in how to conform to proper religious practice. Therefore, the mechanics of how to use this workbook are in service to the larger purpose of this guide: to help those who long after God to become deep people who commit the whole of their lives to the transforming work of the Spirit of Christ.

Remember that throughout your journey, you have the assurance of a Divine Guide, the Holy Spirit, who will be your faithful companion and counselor through every experience along the way. As you consider where and how to position your journey through the Disciplines, draw on the joyful, lifegiving guidance of the Spirit freely bestowed on the children of God.

The most important aspect of using this workbook, therefore, is not simply the determination to "do" the Disciplines and achieve a glow of accomplishment at the end of a particular period of time. Rather, the proper approach to using this guide is a prayerful desire to persist in experiencing a relationship of intimacy with God. It is the determination to walk through the open door to joy and freedom in Christian growth within the community of God's people.

First Quarter:
Overview

The Spiritual Disciplines— Door to Liberation

The Spiritual Disciplines are intended for our good. They are meant to bring the abundance of God into our lives.

Celebration of Discipline, p. 9*

READING: *Celebration of Discipline,* Chapter 1

Reading notes

*Page references for excerpts from *Celebration of Discipline* are to the revised and expanded version (1988).

REFLECTING ON THE SPIRITUAL DISCIPLINES

Read through the chapter in one sitting, and, in the space provided, write down any significant thoughts or questions that occur to you. After you have finished this first reading, take time to gather your thoughts about the journey ahead into a deeper life. You might find it helpful to read the chapter through a second time a little later on, and then return to portions of it throughout the week—as often as time and desire permit—to refresh your thoughts. Use the following questions to help guide your thinking.

- Why are you embarking on this journey into the Disciplines of spiritual growth?

- What are some of the most significant spiritual experiences you have had in the past (positive or negative) that are shaping your expectations or apprehensions in starting this journey?

- What are your hopes for your experiences as you work through this book in the months ahead?

- What are the anxieties or questions you have as you look ahead?

- In what areas of your life are you seeking greater liberation?

A LIGHT FOR THE PATH

In Psalm 42:1–2, the psalmist beautifully expresses one of the most elemental of all human longings:

> As a deer longs for flowing streams,
> so my soul longs for you, O God.
> My soul thirsts for God,
> for the living God.
> When shall I come and behold
> the face of God?

■ How would you describe your own spiritual longings?

> Where the Spirit of the Lord is, there is freedom. . . . But that freedom of Christian living does not come from the human spirit. No human capacities or possibilities or strivings of any kind can achieve this freedom.
> When it happens that man obtains that freedom of becoming a hearer, a responsible, grateful, hopeful person, this is not because of an act of the human spirit, but solely because of the act of the Holy Spirit. So this is, in other words, a gift of God.
>
> KARL BARTH

THE PRACTICE OF THE DISCIPLINES

The Disciplines are means to receiving Divine grace, not exercises in self-improvement. As you begin your journey through the Spiritual Disciplines, take time this week to prepare by affirming God's presence with you.

Consider spending ten minutes in silent listening to God or taking a short "prayer walk." Use any of the following suggestions as you find them helpful for focusing your time with God:

■ Reflect with thanksgiving on the presence of the Spirit in your journey through the Disciplines.

■ Invite God to direct your thoughts regarding your expectations for the journey and where it might lead.

■ Ask God to refresh your perspective on why it is important to practice the Disciplines.

■ Ask God to give you an appropriate orientation of the heart regarding the purposes of your journey.

JOURNAL REFLECTIONS

Use this section to write down your most significant thoughts or experiences from this week, unless you prefer to use a personal journal you may already be keeping. If you would like, use the following "reflection points" as springboards for your thoughts.

■ *Reflection point:* What insights from Foster's discussion of the Spiritual Disciplines are most relevant to you personally? With which do you agree or disagree most strongly?

■ *Reflection point:* What significant experiences, encounters, conversations, or thoughts have you had this week related to your focus on the Spiritual Disciplines?

■ *Reflection point:* Record any significant questions or insights triggered by the questions suggested in "Reflecting on the Spiritual Disciplines" or by the ideas listed in "The Practice of the Disciplines."

The Discipline of Meditation

If we hope to move beyond the superficialities of our culture, including our religious culture, we must be willing to go down into the recreating silences, into the inner world of contemplation.

Celebration of Discipline, p. 15

READING: *Celebration of Discipline,* Chapter 2

Reading notes

REFLECTING ON MEDITATION

Read through the chapter in one sitting, slowly and thoughtfully. Write down any significant insights, comments, or questions that occur to you from the material in the book.

As you read, take time to think about the kinds of meditation described, perhaps envisioning yourself practicing those forms of contemplation. As you reflect on the material in the coming week, use the following questions to help guide your thinking. (Note also "Ideas for Practicing Meditation.")

■ Foster refers to Christian meditation as "the ability to hear God's voice and obey his word." How would you define meditation?

■ What kinds of obstacles to meditation are you most likely to encounter in your daily routines or way of life?

■ For you personally, what are the most important purposes or benefits of meditation?

A LIGHT FOR THE PATH

Psalm 46 is a poetic celebration of the security and comfort promised to God's people. We are encouraged to rest in that knowledge with the profound statement,

> Be still, and know that I am God!

VERSE 10

■ In what ways can you read this declaration as an invitation to meditate?

Our goal in [meditation] is not simply *detachment* from the world but a richer *attachment* to God and to other human beings. As people united with Christ, we seek power and boldness for service in his kingdom. Calvin contended that through meditation on things divine we "may refresh our languishing spirits with new vigor."

DONALD BLOESCH

THE PRACTICE OF MEDITATION

During this overview period, consider "experimenting" with the practice of each Spiritual Discipline during the week in which you are reading the corresponding chapter from *Celebration of Discipline*. In this way you will begin to find out in what senses the Disciplines are easy or hard for you, as well as the unique ways in which they can liberate you to move beyond surface living into the depths of a truly spiritual life.

This experimentation can take varying forms. If you are just starting, select one idea from the following list (or create your own) and implement it at least once this week. If you have already been practicing meditation, you might want to consider a different perspective or approach suggested by your reading, and try that out during the next few days.

Ideas for Practicing Meditation

- Select a Scripture passage to meditate on in the coming week—perhaps the reference cited above or a personal favorite. Write it out on a card you can carry with you, and refer to it often, using spare moments throughout your day to reflect on it. Set aside at least one twenty-minute session for focusing on it prayerfully in greater depth.

- Consecrate one day to seeking opportunities to practice "holy leisure" as a counterpoint to frantic or fragmented activity.

- Identify a particular place that provides a setting of beauty, and spend thirty minutes there contemplating all the ways in which you can see God's gifts to you in it. Or, simply be silent and listen for what God may have to communicate to you. If you desire to, take along a notebook and write down your thoughts.

■ Choose a private spot at home where you can sit comfortably and practice the re-collection exercise Foster describes as "palms down, palms up," or "centering down." Consider using this time to present anxieties or concerns to God.

■ Set aside a session for prayerful meditation on a major aspect of your life, for example: the events of your time and your role in them, a significant relationship or relational context, a vocational desire or pursuit, a form of ministry or social involvement. Seek a deeper clarity and conviction of purpose regarding this area.

INTEGRATING THE DISCIPLINES

In the coming week, you may want to focus primarily on meditation in your practice of the Disciplines. Or, you may want to integrate it in some way with other spiritual practices that are now part of your life. Write down here what you would like to do this week in practicing meditation.

■ Meditation

■ Combined practice of meditation with other Spiritual Disciplines

JOURNAL REFLECTIONS

Write down your most significant thoughts or experiences from this week. If you would like, use the following "reflection points" as springboards for your thoughts.

■ *Reflection point:* What suggestions in Chapter 2 seem most helpful to you in making meditation a regular part of your life?

■ *Reflection point:* If you "experimented" with practicing meditation, describe the experience and any reflections on it that you may have.

■ *Reflection point:* Did you experience any frustrations with the Discipline of meditation? If so, did God teach you anything through these difficulties?

The Discipline of Prayer

It is the Discipline of prayer that brings us
into the deepest and highest work of the
human spirit.

Celebration of Discipline, p. 33

READING: *Celebration of Discipline,* Chapter 3

Reading notes

REFLECTING ON PRAYER

Read through the chapter slowly and thoughtfully, writing down any comments or questions that occur to you. Use the following questions to help guide your thinking about the Discipline of prayer.

■ This chapter primarily focuses on the prayer of *intercession*—asking God to supply the needs of others. What other kinds of prayer do you want to develop more deeply in your life?

■ What are your greatest difficulties in praying?

■ Have you ever sensed an "inner yes" in regard to praying for a particular concern or request? If so, what effect did it have on your prayer?

■ Have you experienced any disappointment with God that causes tension in the way you pray or hinders you from trusting God to answer your prayers?

A LIGHT FOR THE PATH

Reflect on the following key statements from the Scriptures on prayer:

> If you abide in me, and my words abide in you, ask for whatever you wish, and it will be done for you.
>
> JOHN 15:7

> You ask and do not receive, because you ask wrongly, in order to spend what you get on your pleasures.
>
> JAMES 4:3

■ What can you learn from these two declarations about how to pray?

There is a moment between intending to pray and actually praying that is as dark and silent as any moment in our lives. It is the split second between thinking about prayer and really praying. . . . How easy it is, and yet—between us and the possibility of prayer there seems to be a great gulf fixed: an abyss of our own making that separates us from God.

EMILIE GRIFFIN

THE PRACTICE OF PRAYER

Later in this guide you will be returning to the practice of prayer in greater depth. This week, you may want to try out one of the ideas for intercessory prayer from Chapter 3 of *Celebration of Discipline* or simply use any of the insights from your reading to enrich your experience of prayer. (Use the following suggestions if you find them helpful.)

Ideas for Practicing Intercessory Prayer

- Write the preceding two Scripture passages on a card that you can carry through the week with you. Reflect on them often, asking the Spirit to illuminate your understanding of these statements and to open your mind and heart to how they can enrich the way you pray. Consider committing them to memory, so that they can prompt you whenever you spend time in prayer.

- Set aside five to ten minutes each day this week to practice listening for guidance as a prelude to intercessory prayer. Ask God to guide your thoughts and desires toward the people and concerns the Spirit wants you to pray about.

- Ask God to direct your imagination toward a particular person or context in need of healing, envisioning the restoration that God can bring about. Use this imagery to help guide your prayer.

- Practice "flash prayers" as you notice the needs of those around you.

- Practice the re-collection exercise described in Chapter 2 as "palms down, palms up," or "centering down," as a way of praying about anxieties or pressing concerns.

INTEGRATING THE DISCIPLINES

In the coming week, you may want to focus on prayer in your practice of the Disciplines. Or, you may decide to integrate prayer with the Discipline you focused on last week. Write down here how you would like to practice the Disciplines in the coming week.

■   Prayer

■   Combined practice with other Disciplines

JOURNAL REFLECTIONS

Write down your most significant thoughts or experiences from this week. If you would like, use the following "reflection points" as springboards for your thoughts.

- *Reflection point:* What kinds of responses do you have to the Discipline of prayer?

- *Reflection point:* In what aspect of prayer are you least able to feel confident?

- *Reflection point:* What suggestions in Chapter 3 seem most helpful to you in making your experience of prayer more vital? What thoughts, if any, are difficult for you to accept?

- *Reflection point:* What were your experiences of prayer this week? What would you like to reinforce? What would you like to change?

- *Reflection point:* Record your experiences, if any, with the other Disciplines.

The Discipline
of Fasting

Fasting can bring breakthroughs in the
spiritual realm that will never happen in any
other way.

Celebration of Discipline, p. 47

READING: *Celebration of Discipline,* Chapter 4

Reading notes

REFLECTING ON FASTING

Write down any comments or questions that occur to you as you read. Use the following questions to help guide your thinking about the Discipline of fasting.

■ What have your experiences been, if any, with fasting?

■ What kinds of responses do you have to Foster's emphasis on the importance of fasting as an element of Christian devotion?

■ How would you describe the purpose(s) of fasting?

A LIGHT FOR THE PATH

Reflect on the following episode from Jesus' wilderness experience:

> Then Jesus was led up by the Spirit into the wilderness to be tempted by the devil. He fasted forty days and forty nights, and afterwards he was famished. The tempter came and said to him, "If you are the Son of God, command these stones to become loaves of bread." But he answered, "It is written: 'One does not live by bread alone, but by every word that comes from the mouth of God.'"
>
> MATTHEW 4:1–4

■ What insights about fasting does this passage suggest to you?

> Fasting confirms our utter dependence upon God by finding in him a source of sustenance beyond food. Through it, we learn by experience that God's word to us is a life substance, that it is not food ("bread") alone that gives life, but also the words that proceed from the mouth of God (Matt. 4:4). We learn that we too have meat to eat that the world does not know about (John 4:32, 34). Fasting unto our Lord is therefore feasting—feasting on him and on doing his will.
>
> DALLAS WILLARD

THE PRACTICE OF FASTING

If you have never fasted before, you might want to consider experimenting with a brief one this week. If you are experienced with the Discipline of fasting, you might consider a theme or focus suggested by your reading of *Celebration of Discipline*.

Ideas for Practicing Fasting

■ If you have not fasted before, plan a fast of two or more meals' duration— breakfast to breakfast, lunch to lunch, and so on—when you will consume only fruit juice and water. Seek a "gentle receptiveness to divine breathings" during your fast. Afterward, monitor your physical, mental, emotional, and spiritual responses to the fast.

■ If you have fasted before, plan a fast of whatever duration is right for you this week. Perhaps this would be an appropriate time to reflect and pray about your journey into the Spiritual Disciplines in the months ahead.

■ Fast from something that does not involve food—for example, the entertainment media, passing judgment on yourself or others, people (to experience solitude), impulsive speech.

INTEGRATING THE DISCIPLINES

In the coming week, you may want to focus primarily on fasting as an added element in your practice of the Disciplines. Or, you may want to combine fasting with some aspect of meditation or prayer that was especially significant to you in preceding weeks. Make a note here of what you would like to do in practicing the Disciplines.

■ Fasting

Fast once a week for an extended period of time.

■ Combined practice with other Disciplines

JOURNAL REFLECTIONS

Write down your most significant thoughts or experiences from this week. If you would like, use the following "reflection points" as springboards for your thoughts.

- *Reflection point:* If you fasted this week, write down what you did and when. What was the experience like? What changes did you notice from the way you would normally have spent that period of time? Based on this experience, what might you want to change about your practice of fasting to make it more fully centered on God?

- *Reflection point:* What ideas or insights from Chapter 4 are especially challenging, motivating, or helpful to you?

- *Reflection point:* What were your experiences with the other Disciplines?

The Discipline of Study

The purpose of the Spiritual Disciplines is the total transformation of the person. They aim at replacing old destructive habits of thought with new life-giving habits. Nowhere is this purpose more clearly seen than in the Discipline of study.

Celebration of Discipline, p. 62

READING: *Celebration of Discipline,* Chapter 5

Reading notes

REFLECTING ON STUDY

Read through the chapter slowly and thoughtfully, writing down any significant insights. Use the following questions to help you think carefully about the Discipline of study.

■   What kinds of images or experiences does the word *study* conjure up for you?

■   In what ways have you participated in the four components of the Discipline of study—repetition, concentration, comprehension, and reflection—in any area of your life?

■   The reading from *Celebration of Discipline* discusses books, nature, human relationships, self, events, institutions, and cultures as fruitful objects of study. What other areas can you think of that would be appropriate to focus on in the Discipline of study?

■   What forms or methods of study, if any, interest you the most?

A LIGHT FOR THE PATH

Reflect on this important declaration that Jesus made to those who were following his teaching:

> If you continue in my word, you are truly my disciples; and you will know the truth, and the truth will make you free.

JOHN 8:31–32

- What do you think it means to "know" and be "made free" by the truth?

- In what way do you think the Discipline of study enables us to experience the freedom Jesus speaks of here?

To be informed is to know simply that something is the case. To be enlightened is to know, in addition, what it is all about: why it is the case, what its connections are with other facts, in what respects it is the same, in what respects it is different, and so forth.

MORTIMER J. ADLER

THE PRACTICE OF STUDY

In a real sense, you are already engaging in the Discipline of study through your reading of and interaction with *Celebration of Discipline*. Perhaps that is enough for you this week. If you would like to pursue it further, consider the following ideas.

Ideas for Practicing Study

- Choose a brief selection from a book and practice the four steps of repetition, concentration, comprehension, and reflection. Ask yourself, "Do I read to be changed by the truth or to avoid doing the truth?"

- Select a passage of Scripture for a study session. In what ways do you approach, and experience, the Scriptures differently by making a conscious effort to study them, rather than by simply reading them?

- Reflect on your motives, attitudes, or behavior in a particular task or relational mode this week. Apply the Discipline of study as a way of allowing the Spirit to give you increased self-awareness.

- Schedule an interlude in an appropriate location in order to concentrate on studying the book of nature. In what sense does study of nature differ for you from meditation on nature?

- Take time to think through the areas in your life in which the Discipline of study could lead you into a deeper comprehension of truth. Write these down as possibilities for objects of more in-depth study later on in your journey through the Disciplines.

INTEGRATING THE DISCIPLINES

Make a note here of what you would like to do this week in practicing the Disciplines. Use these notations as helpful prompts for what you *want* to do, not guilt-inducing expectations of what you think you *should* do.

■   Study

■   Combined practice with other Disciplines

JOURNAL REFLECTIONS

Write down your most significant thoughts or experiences from this week. If you would like, use the following "reflection points" as springboards for your thoughts.

- *Reflection point:* What have you learned about practicing the Discipline of study in your work on *Celebration of Discipline* so far?

- *Reflection point:* What objects and methods of study seem most suited to your personality, interests, needs, and convictions?

- *Reflection point:* What kinds of experiences did you have this week with other Disciplines—were they helpful or discouraging, enjoyable or disappointing?

The Discipline of Simplicity

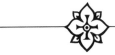

Courageously, we need to articulate new,
more human ways to live.

Celebration of Discipline, p. 81

READING: *Celebration of Discipline,* Chapter 6

Reading notes

REFLECTING ON SIMPLICITY

As you read through the chapter, write down any significant insights. Use the following questions to help you think carefully about the Discipline of simplicity.

■   "Simplicity begins in inward focus and unity," writes Foster. How would you describe your own understanding of God—what Thomas Kelly calls the "divine center"?

■   What things most often get in the way of your living out a simplicity of spirit?

■   What kinds of changes would you most like to make in order to experience "a more human way to live"?

■   How do you think the Discipline of simplicity should affect your attitudes and behavior regarding material possessions?

■   What kinds of inner attitudes and outward expressions do you think are most important for cultivating simplicity? (A helpful reference here is Foster's discussion of the three inner attitudes of simplicity and the ten controlling principles for the outward expression of simplicity.)

A LIGHT FOR THE PATH

Meditate on this classic text from Jesus' Sermon on the Mount:

> Therefore I tell you, do not worry about your life, what you will eat or what you will drink, or about your body, what you will wear. Is not life more than food, and the body more than clothing? Look at the birds of the air; they neither sow nor reap nor gather into barns, and yet your heavenly Father feeds them. Are you not of more value than they? And can any of you by worrying add a single hour to your span of life? And why do you worry about clothing? Consider the lilies of the field, how they grow; they neither toil nor spin; yet I tell you, even Solomon in all his glory was not clothed like one of these. But if God so clothes the grass of the field, which is alive today and tomorrow is thrown into the oven, will he not much more clothe you—you of little faith? Therefore do not worry, saying, "What will we eat?" or "What will we drink?" or "What will we wear?" For it is the Gentiles who strive for all these things; and indeed your heavenly Father knows that you need all these things. But strive first for the kingdom of God and his righteousness, and all these things will be given to you as well.
>
> MATTHEW 6:25–33

■ What kinds of personal responses do you have to this passage?

■ What can you learn about simplicity from Jesus' teaching in this text?

  Christian simplicity is not just a faddish attempt to respond to the ecological holocaust that threatens to engulf us, nor is it born out of a frustration with technocratic obesity. It is a call given to every Christian. The witness to simplicity is profoundly rooted in the biblical tradition, and most perfectly exemplified in the life of Jesus Christ. . . . It is a natural and necessary outflow of the Good News of the Gospel having taken root in our lives.

RICHARD J. FOSTER

THE PRACTICE OF SIMPLICITY

The outward expression of an inward reality is not something you can develop quickly. Since you are in an overview period right now, with only one week per Discipline, you may want to focus your practice of simplicity this week on reflection. The insights you gain can be helpful to you later on in moving through this workbook, when you may decide to spend more time focusing on this Discipline. If you come up with any clear resolves on how you want to pursue the practice of simplicity, consider recording them in the "Record of Commitments" section (page 203).

Here are a few ideas for the coming week.

Ideas for Practicing Simplicity

■ Commit the Scripture passage, Matthew 6:25–33, to memory this week. Meditate on it, pray over it, and write down any resulting thoughts, insights, or questions in your journal reflections.

■ Reflect this week on what Foster identifies as the three inner attitudes of simplicity: (1) receiving what we have as a gift from God; (2) knowing that it is God's business, not ours, to protect what we have; (3) making our goods available to others. Write down your thoughts regarding which of these attitudes would be most helpful for you to focus on in your practice of simplicity.

■ Review Foster's "ten controlling principles" for the outward expression of simplicity. Identify the ones that are most relevant to your life, and write down your thoughts about how you might apply these principles in your circumstances in order to clarify your focus on seeking the kingdom of God first.

■ Set aside an hour-long "separating the wheat from the chaff" session sometime this week. Pray for guidance, and think through major areas of responsibility, commitment, or desire in your life, probing for insight into how the practice of simplicity could help you clarify what is important and weed out what is not. Identify the inward attitudes and outward expressions you want to change or deepen in order to practice the Discipline of simplicity in these areas.

■ Monitor your attitudes and behavior regarding material possessions as you encounter them in your daily activities this week. Write down your observations in your journal reflections.

■ Reflect on your journey through the Spiritual Disciplines in the months ahead as a form of practicing simplicity. Ask yourself such questions as:

- "Am I tempted to take on too much activity?"
- "How can I remain focused in this journey, rather than feeling scattered?"
- "What should I be cutting back on in my life to make room for practicing the Disciplines during this journey?"

INTEGRATING THE DISCIPLINES

Use this section to reflect back on your exposure to the Disciplines thus far. Which ones, if any, do you want to carry into this week with you? Make notations here to prompt your practice.

■ Simplicity

■ Combined practice with other Disciplines

JOURNAL REFLECTIONS

Write down your most significant thoughts or experiences from this week. Use the following "reflection points" as springboards if you find them helpful.

- *Reflection point:* Where are you most vulnerable to duplicity or anxiety—the opposites of simplicity?

- *Reflection point:* In Foster's discussion of simplicity in Chapter 6, what motivated you? What made you concerned or anxious?

- *Reflection point:* Which of the Disciplines you have studied so far seem to be most important to you? Why?

The Discipline of Solitude

Loneliness is inner emptiness. Solitude is inner fulfillment.

Celebration of Discipline, p. 98

READING: *Celebration of Discipline,* Chapter 7

Reading notes

REFLECTING ON SOLITUDE

Read through the chapter and write down your thoughts and responses. Answer any of the following questions that help you reflect on the Discipline of solitude.

- How would you define *solitude* in your own words?

- What kinds of positive and negative images come to your mind with the word *solitude?*

- What do you think are the most important purpose(s) of the Discipline of solitude?

- Have you had any experiences of the "dark night of the soul" described in *Celebration of Discipline?* If so, how did they affect you, and what did you learn from them?

- Where and when have you experienced periods of solitude that provided "inner fulfillment" or "a recreating stillness"?

A LIGHT FOR THE PATH

Reflect on this prophetic declaration given by God to the Israelites through Isaiah:

> For thus saith the Lord God, the Holy One of Israel: In returning and rest shall ye be saved; in quietness and in confidence shall be your strength. . . .

ISAIAH 30:15, KJV

- How does solitude produce confidence?
- How might the truth of this Scripture inform your practice of the Discipline of solitude?

Solitude is the furnace of transformation . . . the place of the great struggle and the great encounter—the struggle against the compulsions of the false self, and the encounter with the loving God who offers himself as the substance of the new self.

HENRI NOUWEN

THE PRACTICE OF SOLITUDE

You may find it helpful this week to focus on solitude "as a state of mind and heart." There are many ways to practice this Discipline even in the midst of a busy schedule. Consider these possibilities.

Ideas for Practicing Solitude

- Look for "little solitudes" among the ordinary experiences of your week. Write down in journal entries when and where you found opportunities, how you spent them, and what difference they made in your day or week.
- Identify a "quiet place" inside or outside your home, and spend a session there this week in which you focus on the fruitfulness of silence.
- Spend a day, or part of a day, without words.
- Be on the alert to any longings for solitude that you experience this week. Write down the circumstances surrounding those longings and consider what prompted them. What do they indicate about your need to practice the Discipline of solitude?
- Take a half-hour silent prayer walk at a nearby park.

INTEGRATING THE DISCIPLINES

Use this section for planning any practice of the Disciplines that you want to engage in this week.

- Solitude

- Combined practice with other Disciplines

JOURNAL REFLECTIONS

Use the following "reflection points" as springboards if you find them helpful in reflecting on your experiences this week.

- *Reflection point:* When do you experience solitude as loneliness or "inner emptiness"?

- *Reflection point:* When do you experience solitude as "inner fulfillment"?

- *Reflection point:* By personality and temperament, are you drawn toward being alone or toward being with people? What does this suggest about your practice of solitude?

- *Reflection point:* Where in your life is silence a healthy practice—for example, to ensure that your words are "few but full," to encourage careful thinking, to be sensitive to others? Where is it an unhealthy practice—for example, because of self-protectiveness, feelings of inadequacy, or fear?

- *Reflection point:* In what ways do you think the Outward Disciplines build on, or are related to, the Inward Disciplines?

  - Meditation
  - Prayer
  - Fasting
  - Study

  - Simplicity
  - Solitude
  - Submission
  - Service

The Discipline of Submission

Every Discipline has its corresponding freedom. What freedom corresponds to submission? It is the ability to lay down the terrible burden of always needing to get our own way.

Celebration of Discipline, p. 111

READING: *Celebration of Discipline,* Chapter 8

Reading notes

REFLECTING ON SUBMISSION

Write down your thoughts and responses as you read through the chapter, using the following questions to help you reflect on the Discipline of submission.

■   Jot down your thoughts quickly and freely on the subject of submission. What words or phrases come to mind? Keep your descriptions brief.

■   What are some of the false or distorted versions of self-denial that masquerade as submission?

■   How is a healthy sense of identity necessary for Christian self-denial?

■   What are some examples of the "limits" of the practice of submission that you might encounter personally?

■   Review the "seven acts of submission" from *Celebration of Discipline.* Would you change this list at all? If so, what changes would you make, and why?

A LIGHT FOR THE PATH

Reflect on this call to deeper living, founded on the life and death of Jesus:

> Do nothing from selfish ambition or conceit, but in humility regard others as better than yourselves. Let each of you look not to your own interests, but to the interests of others. Let the same mind be in you that was in Christ Jesus, who, though he was in the form of God, did not regard equality with God as something to be exploited, but emptied himself, taking the form of a servant, being born in human likeness. And being found in human form, he humbled himself and became obedient to the point of death—even death on a cross.
>
> PHILIPPIANS 2:3–8

■   What insights into submission can you find in this passage?

Father,
I abandon myself into your hands;
do with me what you will.
Whatever you may do, I thank you:
I am ready for all, I accept all.
Let only your will be done in me,
and in all your creatures—
I wish no more than this, O Lord.

CHARLES DE FOUCAULD

THE PRACTICE OF SUBMISSION

Because of the many distortions of this Discipline prevalent in our society—both religious and non-religious—your "experimental" practice this week might take the form of grappling with the concept of submission in order to develop a solid understanding of it. The following suggestions, therefore, emphasize "thinking" through submission as much as "doing" it.

Ideas for Practicing Submission

■ Clarify your points of agreement or disagreement with the material in Chapter 8. Record any lingering questions.

■ Take questions and concerns about submission or self-denial to one or more people you respect and trust. Ask them to talk through these issues with you. Take notes if it is comfortable to do so, and afterward write down summary reflections.

■ List one or more ways you have seen the Discipline of submission used destructively. Consider what caused the incident and how it could be avoided in the future.

■ Make a list of opportunities you have in the course of daily living to give up your own rights for the good of others, and choose one opportunity on which to act this week. Use the suggestions in "The Acts of Submission" (Chapter 8) for specific advice. Afterward, reflect on how this practice of submission helped in any way to free you from the need or desire to have things go the way you want.

INTEGRATING THE DISCIPLINES

Use this section for planning any practice of the Disciplines that you want to engage in this week.

■   Submission

■   Combined practice with other Disciplines

JOURNAL REFLECTIONS

Reflect on your experiences this week, using the following "reflection points" if you find them helpful.

- *Reflection point:* In what areas of your life do you need to develop a clearer understanding of submission?

- *Reflection point:* What fears or anxieties, if any, hinder you from joyfully experiencing the Discipline of submission?

- *Reflection point:* On what areas of your life right now do you want to focus your practice of submission?

- *Reflection point:* What individual or community relationships are you in right now that would benefit from a conscious practice of the Discipline of submission?

- *Reflection point:* What are your greatest difficulties in submitting to God?

The Discipline of Service

True service comes from a relationship with
the divine Other deep inside. We serve out
of whispered promptings, divine urgings.
Energy is expended but it is not the frantic
energy of the flesh.

Celebration of Discipline, p. 128

READING: *Celebration of Discipline,* Chapter 9

Reading notes

REFLECTING ON SERVICE

Write down key thoughts or comments as you read through the chapter, and consider the following questions to help you reflect on the Discipline of service.

■ How would you define the practice of service?

■ In what areas of your life would it especially help you to remember the distinction between "self-righteous" and "true" service?

■ What kinds of "hidden service" do you have opportunity to perform?

■ The final section of Chapter 9 lists at least nine kinds of service. What other types of service have you practiced or received?

■ Which of the nine categories of "service in the marketplace" are already a part of your life? Which would you like to begin, or develop further, in your practice of service?

A LIGHT FOR THE PATH

Set aside time for a slow, careful, and meditative reading of the climactic moment recorded in John 13:1–20 when Jesus washed his disciples' feet and then declared of his act of service,

> For I have set you an example, that you also should do as I have done to you.
>
> VERSE 15

Use the following suggestions to help your reading become an act of intimate fellowship with God.

■ Pray that your reading will become a form of intimate communion with God. Imaginatively place yourself in the event, reading the narrative as if you were actually there as one of the disciples.

■ Ask God to use key words or phrases to stir an inner response in you. If and when that happens, stop reading and meditate on that word or phrase.

■ Pray for insight into what God is teaching you, and for wisdom in applying that insight to your life.

■ After reading the passage at least twice through, contemplate its significance as a whole. Then reflect on any particular insights of personal significance to you that emerged while you were reading. Collect and express your thoughts by writing them down.

Love cannot remain by itself—it has no meaning. Love has to be put into action and that action is service.

MOTHER TERESA

THE PRACTICE OF SERVICE

In the coming week, look for opportunities to practice the Discipline of service in your ordinary routines. Allow any new insights from your reading of Scripture or *Celebration of Discipline* to renew and refresh your joy in serving. Use the following suggestions if you find them helpful.

Ideas for Practicing Service

■ Practice *lectio divina* ("divine reading") with John 13:1–20 by taking several sessions to follow the reading suggestions in "A Light for the Path."

■ Look for opportunities in the coming week to practice the service of small things.

■ Ask God to help you recognize ways in which you are reluctant to submit to others by allowing yourself to be served. Reflect on what this reluctance reveals about your understanding of your relationship to God and your relationships with others.

■ Act on opportunities to practice courtesy this week by looking at them as acts of true Christian service rather than just polite cultural rituals. Reflect on how this perspective affects your experience, if at all.

■ Slow down long enough to practice the service of listening in a context in which you might normally rush on past while preoccupied with tasks, time constraints, or your own needs and obligations.

INTEGRATING THE DISCIPLINES

Use this section for planning any practice of the Disciplines that you want to engage in this week.

■ Service

■ Combined practice with other Disciplines

JOURNAL REFLECTIONS

Reflect on your experiences this week, using the following "reflection points" if you find them helpful.

- *Reflection point:* In what areas of your life do you want to deepen your practice of service?

- *Reflection point:* In what ways, if any, does your actual *practice* of service change your *attitudes* toward service?

- *Reflection point:* Can you experience service as a way of saying no to "the world's games of promotion and authority"? Why or why not?

- *Reflection point:* Which forms of service are hardest for you to practice? Why do you think this is so?

- *Reflection point:* Which acts of service, if any, caused feelings of resentment to surface in you?

- *Reflection point:* Which acts of service made you feel joyful?

The Discipline of Confession

In acts of mutual confession we release the
power that heals. Our humanity is no longer
denied, but transformed.

Celebration of Discipline, p. 146

READING: *Celebration of Discipline,* Chapter 10

Reading notes

REFLECTING ON CONFESSION

Read through the chapter slowly and carefully, writing down any significant questions or insights. Use the following questions as you find them helpful for exploring the Discipline of confession.

■   The importance of confession is built on the assumption that sin (understood in *Celebration of Discipline* as an act or state of living contrary to God's commandments or purposes for our lives or as "offenses to the love of God") is a universal element of the human condition. How do *you* define *sin?*

■   Think back to periods or events in your life that triggered your deepest longings for forgiveness. Did you seek or practice any form of confession? Why or why not?

■   Have you ever had a powerful experience of the cleansing or healing effects of confession? If so, describe how it affected your understanding of yourself in relation to others and to God.

■   In your opinion, when is confession appropriately a private Discipline? When is it appropriately a Discipline practiced in community?

■   Foster recommends these qualifications for those to whom we confess: spiritual maturity, wisdom, compassion, good common sense, the ability keep a confidence, and a wholesome sense of humor. What do you feel is most important in choosing someone who will receive your confession?

A LIGHT FOR THE PATH

Reflect on the following teachings regarding living in fellowship with God and each other:

> This is the message we have heard from him and proclaim to you, that God is light and in him there is no darkness at all. If we say that we have fellowship with him while we are walking in darkness, we lie and do not do what is true; but if we walk in the light as he himself is in the light, we have fellowship with one another, and the blood of Jesus his Son cleanses us from all sin. If we say that we have no sin, we deceive ourselves, and the truth is not in us. If we confess our sins, he who is faithful and just will forgive us our sins and cleanse us from all unrighteousness. If we say that we have not sinned, we make him a liar, and his word is not in us.
>
> 1 JOHN 1:5–10

> Therefore confess your sins to one another, and pray for one another, so that you may be healed.
>
> JAMES 5:16

- What can you learn from these passages about the importance of confession?
- What can you learn from these passages about the practice of confession?

> There is a *higher* experience of repentance, and there is a *deeper* experience of confession of sin than the feeling of regret. In fact, you will find those feelings of regret replaced by something else—replaced by a love and a tranquility. That love, that tranquility sweetly saturates your soul and, having saturated it thoroughly, takes full possession of it.
>
> MADAME JEANNE GUYON

THE PRACTICE OF CONFESSION

This week, be alert to needs or opportunities to practice the Discipline of confession (whether giving or receiving a confession)—without forcing them into expression. For this leg of your journey through the Spiritual Disciplines, it is especially important to draw on relationships with others—a spiritual mentor, a fellowship group, close friends, and so on. The Corporate Disciplines cannot be practiced in isolation from other people. God uses the Christian community as the channel for the freedom we seek.

The following suggestions cover a range of possibilities, since practice of this Discipline will vary according to a variety of individual circumstances and needs.

Ideas for Practicing Confession

■ Set aside time to reflect on your attitudes toward, and practice of, the Discipline of confession. Ask yourself such questions as:

- "Am I in danger of undervaluing this essential element of the Christian life?"
- "Do I have a community of relationships in which I can practice the Corporate Discipline of confession? If not, what should I be doing to develop those relationships?"
- "Have I had any negative experiences that cause me to avoid confession as a Corporate Discipline? If so, how should I be dealing with those experiences in order to gain a healthy perspective?"
- "Am I afraid to examine my life for sin I need to confess? If so, what am I afraid of? How can I let go of this fear?"
- "When I am ready to confess in the presence of another person, do I know to whom I can go? If not, where can I find such a person?"
- "Do I experience the joy that should result from confession? If not, what might be blocking it?"
- "Do I understand and practice the ministry of receiving another's confession and proclaiming the forgiveness of Christ? If not, why not?"

■ Use the approach that Richard Foster devised for practicing confession, detailed in the section "Diary of a Confession." After you have recorded what God reveals to you over a period of at least three days, take it to a trusted friend or mentor who has agreed in advance to listen to your confession and pray with you for receiving the forgiveness of Christ. Afterward, summarize this experience in your journal reflections.

■ During a session of prayer and meditation, seek the Spirit's prompting for any confession God wants you to make—whether to God alone, to a trusted individual, or to a group you may be part of. In preparation for confession, ask yourself these questions:

- "What specific sins do I need to become aware of under the gaze of God?"
- "Am I willing to experience godly sorrow for my sin?"
- "Do I truly yearn to live a holy life?"
- "Do I understand, and am I able to accept, the forgiveness God extends to me?"

■ Ask God to make you aware of any opportunity this week to radiate the light of Christ by receiving another person's confession—in whatever form that unburdening of sin may take. If the opportunity arises, pray for spiritual sensitivity in: listening carefully and quietly; praying inwardly, in the light of the cross, that the other person will receive Christ's love and forgiveness through you; proclaiming the powerful reality of Christ's forgiveness for another personally; praying aloud with him or her for healing the inner wounds of sin; keeping private information private; and responding to how God is ministering to you through this experience.

INTEGRATING THE DISCIPLINES

Use this section for planning your practice of the Disciplines this week.

■ Confession

■ Combined practice with other Disciplines

JOURNAL REFLECTIONS

Use the following "reflection points" as you find them helpful in reflecting on your experiences this week.

- *Reflection point:* Currently, what are your deepest needs for practicing the Discipline of confession?

- *Reflection point:* Where are your greatest difficulties in understanding and accepting the forgiveness of God?

- *Reflection point:* Do you affirm and embrace the reality of what Jesus did for you on the cross, in suffering human sin and redeeming the lost condition of humanity? Why or why not?

- *Reflection point:* In what areas of your life are you in need of experiencing the freedom of community made possible by the common bond of God's Spirit?

- *Reflection point:* Do you understand the common condition of the believing community as a fellowship of sinners? Or do you feel isolated and alone, fearful of revealing what you perceive to be your own failures and shortcomings?

The Discipline of Worship

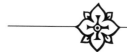

To worship is to experience Reality, to touch
Life . . . we have not worshiped the Lord
until Spirit touches spirit.

Celebration of Discipline, pp. 158–59

READING: *Celebration of Discipline,* Chapter 11

Reading notes

REFLECTING ON WORSHIP

As you read through the chapter, record any questions or comments. Use the following questions to help you reflect on the Discipline of worship.

■   How do you define worship?

■   How important do you think forms and rituals are in the practice of worship?

■   Describe the places and forms in which your experience of worship most often takes place.

■   Genuine worship is sometimes mistakenly identified with the forms created to lead us into it. In what ways, if any, do you tend to practice forms or rituals without genuinely entering the realm where God "touches and frees" your spirit?

■   Review the "Steps into Worship" in *Celebration of Discipline*—at least seven are listed. Would you change or add to this list in any way?

A LIGHT FOR THE PATH

Read the remarkable encounter of Jesus with a Samaritan woman at a well in the heat of midday, recorded in John 4:1–42. Then meditate on the following declaration, one of several profound statements Jesus made to the woman:

> God is spirit, and those who worship him must worship in spirit and truth.

> JOHN 4:24

■   Write down your thoughts and questions about worship as Jesus describes it to the Samaritan woman.

Everything that happens each moment bears the stamp of God's will. How holy is that name! How right to worship it for its own sake! Can we look on him who bears it without infinite reverence? It is celestial manna falling from the sky, pouring down grace; it is the holy kingdom in the soul, it is the bread of angels consumed on earth as it is in heaven. No moment is trivial since each one contains a divine kingdom, and heavenly sustenance.

JEAN-PIERRE DE CAUSSADE

THE PRACTICE OF WORSHIP

Use the following suggestions to guide your practice of worship this week. Seek an opportunity to participate in group or public worship, even if you are not currently a regular member of such a community. The worship that grows out of Christian community is not a right to be demanded but a gift to be graciously received. We cannot force it to happen, but we can prayerfully seek it out.

Ideas for Practicing Worship

- In your next meeting with other believers, practice a "holy expectancy" in preparation for your worship together. How does it affect your participation in worship?

- Practice a "perpetual, inward, listening silence" this week in preparation for corporate worship.

- Choose one simple idea from the "Steps into Worship" listed in Chapter 11 that you think would be especially helpful for your practice of worship. Try out that idea this week, and afterward write down whether and how it affected your worship experience.

- If you are dissatisfied with your participation in corporate worship at this point in your life, choose a trusted friend or mentor who will listen to your concerns and reflect back to you any helpful comments or questions to direct you toward appropriate paths for growth in this area.

INTEGRATING THE DISCIPLINES

Write down any notes here for your practice of the Disciplines this week.

■   Worship

■   Combined practice with other Disciplines

JOURNAL REFLECTIONS

Use the following "reflection points" to stimulate your thoughts about your journey in the Discipline of worship.

- *Reflection point:* Are there any changes you would like to make in your current patterns of practicing worship?

- *Reflection point:* How would you characterize your strongest and weakest areas in the Discipline of worship?

- *Reflection point:* Are there any areas in which you feel the Holy Spirit may be prompting you to renewed spiritual responsiveness in your worship? If so, what mode or form of worship might be an appropriate expression for it?

- *Reflection point:* Are you currently part of a community of believers in which you can experience the *koinonia* of corporate worship?

    If not, what would it take for you to become part of such a group?

    If so, are you satisfied with the contribution you are making to the spiritual health and vitality of that group?

The Discipline of Guidance

Unity rather than majority rule is the
principle of corporate guidance. Spirit-given
unity goes beyond mere agreement. It is the
perception that we have heard the *Kol
Yahweh*, the voice of God.

Celebration of Discipline, p. 182

READING: *Celebration of Discipline,* Chapter 12

Reading notes

REFLECTING ON GUIDANCE

Read through the chapter carefully, writing down any significant insights or questions. The following questions offer suggestions for reflecting on the Discipline of guidance.

■ Write down your thoughts in the columns below about the unique strengths and liabilities of seeking God's guidance in community versus individually.

	Strengths	Liabilities
Seeking God's guidance in community		
Seeking God's guidance individually		

■ Have you ever received guidance from God through an individual (or individuals) who ministered to you in the capacity of a spiritual director or mentor?

   If so, what were the highlights of that experience? What were the disappointments, if any, of that experience?

   If not, is this relationship something you desire to have now? Why or why not?

■ Check your level of comfort or discomfort with the following forms of spiritual direction and guidance.

	Very Comfortable	Somewhat Comfortable	Not sure	Somewhat Uncomfortable	Very Uncomfortable
A formally established community of believers, with clearly structured organization and authority	☐	☐	☐	☐	☐
An informally gathered community of believers, with spontaneous and fluid lines of organization and authority	☐	☐	☐	☐	☐
A spiritual director	☐	☐	☐	☐	☐
A network of trusted friends with common commitments and shared beliefs	☐	☐	☐	☐	☐
Preaching	☐	☐	☐	☐	☐
Small group ministry	☐	☐	☐	☐	☐
Bible reading and study	☐	☐	☐	☐	☐

Are you satisfied with all the responses you checked? Or do any of those responses suggest areas in which you would like to change your practice of corporate guidance?

■ Chapter 12 lists the following limits of corporate guidance: manipulation and control by leaders; group opposition to Spirit-inspired leadership; departure from, or distortion of, biblical norms in corporate guidance; disruption of unity by basic human shortcomings or differences. Have you come up against any of these limits in your experience? What kinds of responses did you have?

A LIGHT FOR THE PATH

Reflect on the following declaration Jesus made regarding believers in community:

> Again, truly I tell you, if two of you agree on earth about anything you ask, it will be done for you by my Father in heaven. For where two or three are gathered in my name, I am there among them.

MATTHEW 18:19–20

■ Why do you think "agreement" between believers is so important that Jesus places it as a condition of the Father's response?

■ Do you think these statements mean that Jesus' presence in a group gathered in his name differs in some unique way from his presence with individuals? Why or why not?

> . . . we come now to the question as to how God's guidance is to come to us, and how we shall be able to know His voice. There are four ways in which He reveals His will to us—through the Scriptures, through providential circumstances, through the convictions of our own higher judgment, and through the inward impressions of the Holy Spirit on our minds. Where these four harmonize, it is safe to say that God speaks.

HANNAH WHITALL SMITH

THE PRACTICE OF GUIDANCE

Receiving divine guidance through other believers is not something we can simply set out to accomplish. It is a gift we receive at God's initiative—often in the context of relationships established over time.

However, we *can* decide to reflect on such issues as: our openness or reluctance to receiving guidance; whether we seek or avoid contexts in which we can receive such guidance; our desire to be a committed member of a "community of loving persons."

Consider these suggestions for practicing the Discipline of guidance in the coming week.

Ideas for Practicing Guidance

■ Set aside time to reflect on your receptivity to receiving guidance through others. Ask yourself, "In what areas am I open to God's leading in community? In what areas am I reluctant or fearful to experience divine guidance in community?"

■ Spend time examining ways in which you do or do not place yourself in a position that will allow you to receive the gift of corporate guidance. Does your reflection suggest any changes you want to make? How might you approach making those changes?

■ Take a personal inventory of the ways in which you receive spiritual direction. Then ask yourself:

- "Are there any areas I want to strengthen? What steps can I take to do so?"
- "Are there any relationships in which I am currently involved that have become unhealthy and lost their potential to provide spiritual direction? How should I respond when I come up against the limits of corporate guidance in this case?"

■ Think of someone with whom you might want to develop an ongoing relationship of mutual spiritual direction. Take him or her out to lunch to get better acquainted.

INTEGRATING THE DISCIPLINES

Write down any notes here for your practice of the Disciplines this week.

■ Guidance

■ Combined practice with other Disciplines

JOURNAL REFLECTIONS

Use the following "reflection points" to stimulate your thoughts about your experiences with the Discipline of guidance.

■ *Reflection point:* In what areas of your life, if any, have you experienced the most growth through divine guidance in the context of community?

■ *Reflection point:* Look back on major decisions, struggles, adjustments, or periods of change in your life. Can you identify any places in which you wish you had sought corporate guidance or in which you missed opportunities to be helped by those who could have provided loving, wise direction for you? What can you learn from these experiences that will help you grow toward a more vital participation in community?

■ *Reflection point:* What experiences have you had, if any, in which you were disappointed, disillusioned, or hurt by human distortions, failings, or betrayals—in conflict with the trust you had placed in the ministry of a believing community? How have these experiences shaped your current attitudes toward, or practice of, the Discipline of guidance?

■ *Reflection point:* Are there any areas in which you sense the Holy Spirit prompting you to strengthen, renew, or clarify your practice of the Discipline of corporate guidance?

The Discipline of Celebration

Without joyous celebration to infuse the other
Disciplines, we will sooner or later abandon
them. Joy produces energy. Joy makes us
strong.

Celebration of Discipline, p. 191

READING: *Celebration of Discipline,* Chapter 13

Reading notes

REFLECTING ON CELEBRATION

As you read through this final chapter, write down your responses. Use the following questions as you find them helpful for reflecting on the Discipline of celebration.

■   How often do you experience real joy in your life?

    □   Very often
    □   Every now and then
    □   On rare occasions
    □   Hardly ever
    □   Never
    □   Not sure

■   "Celebration is central to all the Spiritual Disciplines. . . . Every Discipline should be characterized by carefree gaiety and a sense of thanksgiving." Reflect on this statement by answering the following questions about it:

    What is your immediate, first response to this statement?
    To what extent has this been your experience so far in your journey with *Celebration of Discipline?*
    If you had fully grasped this perspective when just starting your overview of the Disciplines, do you think it would have made a difference in your approach to them? Why or why not?

■   In what ways, if any, have you experienced obedience as the path to joy?

■   Are there any ways in which disobedience has robbed you of joy?

A LIGHT FOR THE PATH

"Rejoice in the Lord" is one of St. Paul's refrains in his epistle to the Philippians. This particular recurrence of it is followed by a profound "how-to":

> Rejoice in the Lord always; again I will say, Rejoice. Let your gentleness be known to everyone. The Lord is near. Do not worry about anything, but in everything by prayer and supplication with thanksgiving let your requests be made known to God. And the peace of God, which surpasses all understanding, will guard your hearts and your minds in Christ Jesus.

PHILIPPIANS 4:4–7

- What kind of celebration does Paul call believers to in this passage?

- How do you think the other Spiritual Disciplines can help release the joy and peace Paul describes?

> As we crossed the threshold of the final decade of the twentieth century, we found ourselves inundated with images of dramatic change and flickering hope . . . images of young people dancing on the Berlin Wall . . . children singing in the streets of Soweto at the release of Nelson Mandela . . . Hungarian students crowding into churches to pray. . . . I strongly affirm that these flickers of hope are neither random nor isolated. The jubilant dancing on the Berlin Wall is the dance of God. The songs of freedom sung exuberantly by South African children are the songs of God. The ardent prayers of East European young people are the prayers of God.

TOM SINE

THE PRACTICE OF CELEBRATION

As you think about how you would like to practice celebration this week, remember that it is a Corporate Discipline. Look for ways to share the joy of God with others. Here are some suggestions.

Ideas for Practicing Celebration

- Celebrate your journey through the Spiritual Disciplines thus far by sharing with another person, or group of persons, the joys and frustrations of your experiences in recent weeks and months.

■ Choose a person you know who best expresses a "spirit of carefree celebration," or whose life seems to be characterized by a genuine joy in the Lord. Ask that person to spend some time (at least one hour-long session) with you discussing this aspect of living. Take with you such questions as: "What enables you to live in such a carefree way? How do you experience the joy of the Lord in the midst of the sadness and struggle of life? What have you learned about living that has changed your understanding of obedience, joy, praise, or celebration?"

■ Get together with one or more friends sometime this week simply for relaxation and pleasure. Celebrate the simple goodness of life: find a place to play and then lose yourselves in fun; watch a funny movie; mock your own seriousness; tell silly jokes; have a good laugh.

■ Pick one creative activity to do with family or friends: throw a party for any reason—or for no reason; play a game, indoors or outdoors; playact an event, or satirize your usual routine and patterns; sketch, paint, or sculpt together; write a story together and then read it to someone; plant something in your home or yard; have a vocal or instrumental jam session; do something in preparation for celebrating an upcoming season, holiday, or sacred occasion.

INTEGRATING THE DISCIPLINES

Write down any notes here for your practice of the Disciplines this week.

■ Celebration

■ Combined practice with other Disciplines

JOURNAL REFLECTIONS

Use the following "reflection points" to stimulate your thoughts about your experiences with the Discipline of celebration.

- *Reflection point:* What is easy for you to celebrate in your life right now?

- *Reflection point:* What is difficult for you to celebrate in your life right now—that is, the mourning that will not yield to dancing?

- *Reflection point:* In what ways are joy and laughter part of your life?

- *Reflection point:* What have been some of the most profound ways in which you have experienced the joy of the Lord in community?

- *Reflection point:* Which experiences in your journey through the Spiritual Disciplines so far would you like to celebrate?

- *Reflection point:* As you look ahead to more in-depth practice of the Spiritual Disciplines, where do you especially want to focus on a "joyful spirit of festivity"?

Second Quarter:
The Inward
Disciplines

Reflection and Evaluation

Now that you have read through *Celebration of Discipline* and spent time exploring each of the Spiritual Disciplines, this is a natural turning point for rest, celebration, and reflection on your experiences so far.

During this "hinge week," use the suggestions provided to help you take stock, get perspective, and evaluate where you would like to set your sights in the months ahead. You might find it more comfortable to work through this planning week in several sessions, rather than trying to do it all at once. Feel free to slow the pace down by taking several weeks for the reflection and evaluation activities presented here. Move on to the Inward Disciplines when you feel mentally, emotionally, and spiritually ready to do so.

CELEBRATION

Before you move ahead into a more in-depth exploration of the Disciplines, take time to celebrate the experiences of the first thirteen weeks of your journey. Either alone or with friends, spend an hour or more thanking God for what you have learned thus far (and anticipating the discoveries of the months ahead).

This session could take any form: a solitary interlude for reflection and writing, perhaps composing a prayer or poem to mark this passage point; an outdoor activity to refresh mind, body, and spirit with enjoyment of creation; a special meal that you prepare with others; an informal worship service of communion and praise. Allow this celebration to encourage within you a "carefree gaiety and sense of thanksgiving."

STRUCTURE OF THE WORKBOOK

From here on, this workbook will offer you a more flexible format that you can personalize as you wish.

The rest of the year is divided into quarters, each one focusing on one group of Disciplines: Inward, Outward, and Corporate. Introducing each of these groups is a hinge week of reflection like the one you are in now.

Following this hinge week, each quarter contains in-depth sections with ideas for practicing the respective Disciplines. These sections are set up with questions for further reading and reflection on the Disciplines, specific suggestions for practice, Scripture passages and literary quotations to contemplate, and "reflection points" for journal entries.

If you focus three weeks of in-depth exploration on each Discipline, you will move through the next three quarters at a steady pace: each quarter will have one initial week of reflection followed by twelve weeks spread over the four Disciplines in that quarter. However, you may want to spend more time on one Discipline than another, and so the structure of this workbook is set up to give you that flexibility.

You might also choose a different approach to the in-depth exploration by jumping ahead to other Disciplines or changing the order in which you focus on them. You may decide to dwell on a particular Discipline or cluster of Disciplines for as long as you feel called to do so, rather than assigning a particular number of weeks. Or you may be in a particular season of the year with unique opportunities and needs. The suggested structure of this workbook is intended to support your journey, not control it. As you become familiar with the contents, adapt them to your own needs and circumstances.

Remember that the purpose of our practice of the Disciplines is a greater intimacy with God, and flowing from that intimacy a freer and more joyful life of faith. It is not to become adept at religious practices, nor is it to achieve a gratifying accomplishment by fulfilling a rigid set of performance expectations or checking off items on a do-list. We are called to feast on God, not indulge in spiritual gluttony by trying to squeeze in as much as possible. The mechanics of practice, and indeed the Disciplines themselves, are only the means to an end. Let this reality free you to enjoy your journey, rather than allowing it to become a superstructure of expectations or demands.

A reminder from Chapter 1 of *Celebration of Discipline* is helpful here: It is possible to turn the Disciplines into "another set of soul-killing laws." Our journey is along "the path of disciplined grace"—"'grace' because it is free" and "'disciplined' because there is something for us to do."

In this context, the "Record of Commitments" (page 203) is provided as a handy reference point for the decisions you make regarding ongoing practice. If, for example, you decide you want to fast once a month, or set aside a few months from the year ahead for studying a particular topic or book, then write it down in this section. Keeping a record of your commitments in this way will serve two purposes: (1) you will have a quickly accessible reference for weekly planning because you can see in one glance what your desires are for all the Disciplines, not just those on which you are currently focusing, and (2) you will have a tool for evaluating whether you are taking on too much.

LOOKING BACK

As you are ready to look back at the preceding quarter, work through the following questions to help you evaluate your experiences. Feel free to skip any questions for which you lack time or interest.

- Briefly describe your overall impressions of the Spiritual Disciplines based on your experiences to date.

- Which Disciplines seemed most enjoyable or significant to you?

- Which Disciplines seemed least enjoyable or significant to you?

- What were the most important insights you learned about yourself and your relationships?

■ What were the most important insights you learned about God or about the nature of your relationship with God?

■ What changes, if any, have you noticed in your perceptions of or attitudes toward the Disciplines as a path to deeper living?

■ How would you describe the high points or deepest satisfactions of your experiences in the preceding weeks?

■ How would you describe the chief struggles or frustrations of your experiences in the preceding weeks?

LOOKING AHEAD

Based on your evaluations above, work through the following questions to help you consider how to focus your journey through the Inward Disciplines in the next twelve weeks. Answer those questions that seem most helpful to you in gathering your thoughts.

■ What personal desires and concerns regarding your spiritual growth do you want to address in the weeks ahead?

■   Which Inward Disciplines are you most eager to develop more deeply in the months ahead?

■   Which positive experiences from the past thirteen weeks do you want to build on?

■   What do the struggles or disappointments of the past thirteen weeks indicate about how you should be planning for practice in the next three months?

■   Look back at your notes and journal entries from Weeks 2 through 5. Are there any specific practices of the Inward Disciplines you experimented with during those weeks that you want to incorporate in the second quarter?

■   Take time to reflect on any commitments to ongoing practice of the Spiritual Disciplines that you feel ready to make at this point. (If you do not feel ready to make such commitments, don't force yourself to do so. Wait until you have had opportunity to explore the Disciplines in greater depth before you decide on consistent forms of practicing them.) These commitments may have arisen from your experimentation with the Disciplines during the first quarter, or they may originate in practices that have been part of your life for many years, which you carried with you into this journey. Consider these commitments with careful thought and prayer, perhaps also in consultation with others who can help advise you. Then enter them in the "Record of Commitments" section of this workbook (see page 203).

PLANNING FOR THE SECOND QUARTER

If you follow the suggested structure and allot three weeks for each Inward Discipline, you will move through the second quarter in four equal segments as shown in the planning chart that follows. This doesn't necessarily mean that you will do nothing with the other Disciplines during a given three-week period; the time assignments simply show where your main focus will be.

You may want to focus your practice differently than the suggested structure and spend more time on one Discipline while reducing the number of weeks for another. Take time now to consider this decision with careful thought and prayer. You might also talk it over with a spiritual companion, close friend, or support group who can help you clarify how God is leading you. Then give yourself the freedom to chart your own path for this part of the journey.*

If you are exploring these Disciplines in a group context, make the decision a matter of group discussion and prayer. You may decide that each group member will personalize this decision according to need and interest. However, the simple act of discussing it together will stimulate and enrich your planning. In the right-hand column of the following chart, note any changes in how you want to structure your weeks with the Inward Disciplines. (You might want to pencil in these notations. Over the coming weeks you may end up following this plan exactly, or you may change direction as experiences and the guidance of the Spirit lead you into new insights.)

---

*Keep in mind that sometimes the Disciplines we like the least or struggle with the most are the ones that especially need our concentrated attention, as an athlete strives to improve weak areas rather than avoid them. We should keep this possibility in tension with other factors such as natural inclination and personal interests.

Suggested structure	Week	Alternative structure
Meditation	15	
	16	
	17	
Prayer	18	
	19	
	20	
Fasting	21	
	22	
	23	
Study	24	
	25	
	26	

Once you begin to work through the ideas for practicing each of the Inward Disciplines, consider taking time each week to step back from your activity and assess where you are. A weekly half-hour review will help you clarify your perspective and keep it fresh (for specific suggestions, see "Ideas for Weekly Planning"). If you use these sessions as "time out" to take a breather from activities, gain perspective on your experiences, and reflect on the appropriate pace and focus for your planning, you will be less likely to feel lost or overwhelmed.

The best method for taking these steps back each week is to keep a journal separate from this workbook. If you are not already maintaining a personal journal, pick up a spiral-bound notebook in a convenient size. Use your journal to reflect on how you feel God is leading you to focus your practice of the Disciplines and where your journey is taking you.

HEADING INTO EACH DISCIPLINE

As you head into the specific Disciplines, take time to get an overall perspective on how you want to focus your practice. As you begin each section, follow these four steps to maximize the benefit of the ideas for in-depth exploration of each Inward Discipline:

1. Read through the ideas listed and familiarize yourself with them. Circle or check those you think you want to use.
2. Refer back to your planning chart to refresh your memory regarding how many weeks you want to spend with this Discipline.
3. Set goals, based on the ideas you circled or checked, for what you want to do each week. If you would rather not keep these goals in your head, write them down in your journal—perhaps assigning weekly pages for the duration of your focus on this Discipline, with the goals as the headings.

   This exercise will establish a helpful target, even if you shift your specific focus during a given week.
4. Review your "Record of Commitments" for your intentions regarding ongoing practice of other Disciplines. If you desire to integrate any goals listed there with your exploration of meditation in coming weeks, make a note of those goals on the appropriate pages in your journal.

Once you have taken these four steps, you will be well prepared to head into each Inward Discipline with at least an initial direction for how you want to proceed.

IDEAS FOR WEEKLY PLANNING

At the start of each week, perhaps on Sunday evenings, spend a half-hour getting perspective on where you are in your journey. Your journal will be an invaluable support for this time by giving you a place to write down your reflections and plans. You might simply mark a new page with "Weekly Planning" and the date, so later on you can go back and find it easily.

Here are a few ideas for how to make good use of this weekly review:

1. Take a mini-break by mentally stepping back from your progress through the Spiritual Disciplines. Pause to thank God for grace for the journey.
2. Reflect on the significance of your experiences in the preceding week (the "reflection points" listed at the end of each individual Discipline section are intended for this purpose).

3. Check back to your overall plan for the second quarter that you sketched out in the planning chart. If you want to shift the time frames you decided on earlier, change the chart accordingly. Also, check your "Record of Commitments" for practice of other Disciplines you want to carry into the week, writing it down if you find it helpful to do so.

4. Review your responses to the questions you answered in the "Looking Ahead" section earlier in this session. Make note of any desires or commitments you want to carry forward into the coming week. If you have assigned weekly pages and written down goals for practicing the current Discipline, review those goals and adjust them if necessary.

5. Throughout the week, keying off your weekly goals, work through the material you have circled or checked in each section. Proceed at whatever pace is comfortable for you. There is plenty of space in the individual in-depth Discipline sections for you to take notes and record your experiences, but you may find it helpful to record key insights or events in your journal as they occur during the week.

WRAPPING UP HINGE WEEK 14

In your journal or in the space provided here, note any additional thoughts and reflections from this planning week.

Celebrating Meditation

> In meditation . . . the perpetual presence of
> the Lord (omnipresence, as we say) moves
> from a theological dogma into a radiant
> reality. "He walks with me and talks with
> me" ceases to be pious jargon and instead
> becomes a straightforward description of daily
> life.
>
> *Celebration of Discipline,* p. 19

SUGGESTIONS FOR FURTHER READING OF
CELEBRATION OF DISCIPLINE, Chapter 2

■   Look up the Scripture passages Foster refers to (and any others you may want
    to study) as part of the "Biblical Witness" to the practice of meditation. Write
    down observations, questions, and insights as you read through these Scrip-
    tures. Then, as a way of collecting your thoughts, write a summary paragraph
    describing meditation based on these biblical sources.

■ In Foster's discussion of meditation as "Hearing and Obeying," what insights does he provide into what it means to be intimate with God?

■ Have you ever held any of the views of meditation described in "Understandable Misconceptions"? If so, which ones? How has your reading and/or practice in your journey so far helped you dispel any of them?

■ What ideas can you find in this chapter that can help you "sanctify" your imagination as part of your practice of meditation?

■ Review Foster's distinction between meditation and study in Chapter 5 (first edition, pp. 55–56; revised edition, p. 64). What further insights into meditation can you find there?

SPECIFIC SUGGESTIONS FOR PRACTICING THE DISCIPLINE OF MEDITATION

Use the following ideas as you find them helpful for practicing meditation. You might want to start by referring back to your notes from Week 2, or to any other practice of meditation you may have done in the thirteen weeks of overview, and picking up where you left off. Also, review the specific suggestions and advice in Chapter 2 of *Celebration of Discipline*.

■ Select one or more Scripture passages (possibly selected from the list below, from any current Bible reading you may be doing, or simply from your own personal favorites) to meditate on in the coming weeks, perhaps one each week. How does your understanding of the truth in these passages change or deepen as a result of your meditation on it?

Another suggestion for meditating on Scripture is through imaginative participation in one of the events of Jesus' life recorded in the Gospel narratives as you seek to be "initiated into the reality of which the passage speaks." For example, you might place yourself:

- as one of the many individuals Jesus healed
- as one of the disciples on the Mount of Transfiguration (Matt. 17:1–3, Mark 9:2–12, Luke 9:28–36)
- as Mary or Martha at the death of their brother Lazarus (John 11)
- as the Samaritan woman at the well (John 4:1–26)
- as one of the disciples during Christ's post-resurrection appearances—on the beach when the disciples returned from fishing (John 21) or on the road as the disciples walked from Jerusalem to Emmaus (Luke 24:13 ff.)
- as the child who gave away his lunch at the feeding of the five thousand (John 6:1–15)
- as Peter, in denying Jesus (John 13:36–38, 18:15–27)
- as Mary, watching her son die on the cross (John 19:25–27)
- as Mary Magdalene, in the garden after Jesus' death (John 20:10–18)

■ Set aside one day per week to engage in "holy leisure." Seek to integrate a meditative way of life in your daily routines over the week(s) that you engage in this practice. Reflect on your experiences with this practice by considering: "How can I continue to replace frantic activity with holy leisure in my daily life?"

■ Focus on practicing meditation on nature over the next several weeks. Identify and capitalize on opportunities—whether carefully planned or brief and spontaneous. Keep a notebook with you to record thoughts and experiences as they occur. Be alert to how this practice can train your inward eye for sharper observation and appreciation of God's creation.

■ Practice meditation on people by paying close attention to behavior, attitudes, moods, and responses in the ordinary circumstances and encounters of your daily routines. Reflect on these observations:

- regarding others—"Why do they speak and act the way they do?"
- regarding yourself—"Why did I say that? Why am I acting this way?"

■ Incorporate the practice of "palms down, palms up" (also called "re-collection" or "centering down") on its own or as preparation for prayer; do this daily or several times per week. You might want to select a focus for these times, such as: presentation of concerns and anxieties—whether personal, communal, or global—to God; intercession for friends and loved ones; intercession for world events and the work of God's kingdom around the world; and so on.

■ Once a week, or more frequently, schedule a session of meditation on a major aspect of your life. For example: the events of your time and your role in them; a significant relationship or relational context; a vocational desire or pursuit; a form of ministry or social involvement; an area of struggle or growth in greater self-knowledge; the need for direction in specific decisions you must make; desire for behavioral or attitudinal change; stamina, endurance, grace, or wisdom for trials or difficulties you may be facing. Keep a written record of how your meditation impacts this area over the weeks that you continue the practice.

SCRIPTURE PASSAGES RELEVANT TO THE PRACTICE OF MEDITATION

The following Scripture passages are just a few of the many biblical texts providing insights into the practice of meditation.

■ Psalm 8 is a model for meditation on the glory of God revealed in the creation. (See also Psalm 19.)

■ Psalm 46:10 provides insight into the nature and focus of meditation.

■ Psalm 119 is a rich collection of meditations on the Word of God, suggestive for the practice as well as the benefits of meditation. You might want to select a few stanzas, or perhaps the repeated refrain of delight in God's commandments.

■ Matthew 26:36–46 records Jesus' meditation in the Garden of Gethsemane, revealing his responses to one of the most anguished moments of his life.

■ John 16:12–15 describes the presence and ministry of our Divine Guide, the Holy Spirit. (See also the insights into the ministry of the Spirit in 1 Corinthians 2.)

■ Romans 8:1–17 emphasizes the importance of the human mind and spirit in contrasting life in the Spirit with subjection to sin and death.

■ Revelation 3:20 records Christ's invitation to intimacy, the heart of meditation.

THOUGHTS FOR CONTEMPLATION

Reflect on the following quotations to stimulate and inform your practice of meditation.

Contemplative prayer is, in a way, simply the preference for the desert, for emptiness, for poverty. One has begun to know the meaning of contemplation when he intuitively and spontaneously seeks the dark and unknown path of aridity in preference to every other way.

THOMAS MERTON

Love desires to dwell at peace in the presence of the beloved. So the contemplative is advised not to be restlessly searching, turning over new ideas. . . . Contemplation learns, moreover, to draw nourishment from less and less material as time goes on, as its ability grows to see and grasp depth and totality in the individual fragment. Sooner or later, by grace, it will be brought to the "prayer of quiet," a prayer in which extension is replaced by the intensive dimension; the unstable, wide-ranging, discursive element of thought is replaced by a kind of intuition which takes in far more, at a single glance, than the beginner's roving eye.

HANS URS VON BALTHASAR

May I hasten to say that the kind of prayer I am speaking of is not a prayer that comes from your mind. It is a prayer that begins in the heart. . . . Prayer offered to the Lord from your mind simply would not be adequate. Why? Because your mind is very limited. The mind can pay attention to only one thing at a time. Prayer that comes out of the heart is not interrupted by thinking! I will go so far as to say that nothing can interrupt this prayer, *the prayer of simplicity.*

MADAME JEANNE GUYON

The time of business does not with me differ from the time of prayer; and in the noise and clatter of my kitchen, while several persons are at the same time calling for different things, I possess God in as great tranquillity as if I were upon my knees at the blessed sacrament.

BROTHER LAWRENCE

REFLECTION POINTS FOR JOURNAL ENTRIES

In addition to recording your experiences from any of the questions or practices previously suggested, you may find the following "reflection points" helpful as a way of chronicling your journey into the Discipline of meditation.

- *Reflection point:* How is the practice of meditation leading you into a deeper experience of intimacy with God?
- *Reflection point:* What do you enjoy most about the practice of meditation?
- *Reflection point:* What are your greatest struggles or disappointments in practicing meditation?
- *Reflection point:* What has your practice of meditation been teaching you about yourself and your relationships?
- *Reflection point:* What has your practice of meditation been teaching you about God?
- *Reflection point:* Where does meditation seem to integrate most naturally with any of the other Spiritual Disciplines in your own practice?
- *Reflection point:* Which forms of practicing meditation do you think you are most likely to continue in the future, once you have moved beyond this workbook?

Celebrating Prayer

Meditation introduces us to the inner life,
fasting is an accompanying means, study
transforms our minds, but it is the Discipline
of prayer that brings us into the deepest and
highest work of the human spirit. Real prayer
is life creating and life changing.

Celebration of Discipline, p. 33

SUGGESTIONS FOR FURTHER READING OF
CELEBRATION OF DISCIPLINE, Chapter 3

■   Review the references early in the chapter to those who "viewed prayer as the main business of their lives"—Martin Luther, John Wesley, David Brainerd, and others. Reflect on Foster's comment, "For those explorers in the frontiers of faith, prayer was no little habit tacked onto the periphery of their lives; it *was* their lives." What can you learn from these individuals—despite any potential discouragement you might feel?

(For additional reading, consider obtaining biographical resources on one or more of these individuals. Read meditatively in order to stimulate your prayer life.)

- Review Foster's discussion of using or not using the phrase "If it be thy will" in the section "Learning to Pray." Do you agree with his positions? Why or why not? Ask a few other people, whom you consider models for the practice of prayer, to give you their responses. Allow their insights to inform your own.

- Review the analogy of the TV set in determining what may be blocking our prayer (first edition, p. 34; revised edition, p. 38). Do you agree with the point made here that "we can know that our prayers are being answered as surely as we can know that the television set is working"? Why or why not?

- Reread Foster's account of praying for a seriously ill baby girl with her preschool-age brother (first edition, p. 37; revised edition, pp. 41–42). How do you feel about the fact that they thanked God in advance for the healing they assumed would occur in answer to their prayer? Would you pray in this way with a child, especially about someone at the center of that child's life? Why or why not?

- Review the discussion of contemplative prayer in Chapter 2 of *Celebration of Discipline*, located in the section "The Forms of Meditation." What insights from the Discipline of meditation can enrich your understanding of prayer?

SPECIFIC SUGGESTIONS FOR PRACTICING THE DISCIPLINE OF PRAYER

The following ideas build on those listed in Week 3 for practicing intercessory prayer. As you look ahead, review your practice of the Discipline of prayer in recent weeks. You may want to pick up a particular approach and continue developing it; address an area of struggle in prayer by working on it further instead of avoiding it; or combine your practice of prayer with another closely related Discipline, such as meditation or fasting.

Use the suggestions listed here to guide your journey. You might find it helpful to maintain a dialogue with others, or a trusted spiritual adviser, regarding your plans. Also, hold this work lightly, allowing yourself a periodic "break" from these prayer experiments to guard against taking in more than you can reasonably digest.

- Select one or more Scripture passages that enrich your understanding of prayer, motivate you to pray, or present models or forms of prayer that you want to incorporate. Review them frequently, commit them to memory, and pray that the Spirit would illuminate your heart and mind with their truth. During time that you set aside for prayer, use them to usher yourself into prayer or to shape and inform the way that you pray. (See "Scripture Passages Relevant to the Practice of Prayer" for suggestions regarding specific references.)

- Choose a good book on prayer to refresh and stimulate your practice. Read slowly and reflectively, one portion at a time, while concurrently spending as much or more time actually praying. Do not let reading become a substitute for praying.

  If you would like a reading list, start with the works referenced in *Celebration of Discipline* (first edition: see "Notes," especially pp. 173–75; revised edition: see "Notes," especially pp. 211–12, and the annotated bibliography on pp. 217–21).

- Deepen your practice of intercessory prayer by choosing a few individuals or groups for whom you will pray in an intensified way in coming weeks and months. (If you make a commitment here, write it down in your "Record of Commitments" on page 203.) Establish a schedule of prayer times, and write down very specific requests, changing or adjusting those requests as is appropriate during the duration of your intensified intercession for them. During these prayer times, seek God's leading by listening for divine guidance regarding the nature of the prayer you are about to offer, perhaps in the form of a mental picture of what the Spirit desires to do in this person's life.

  Ask God to deepen your sensitivity to these persons over the course of time. Apply the Discipline of study to heighten your awareness of their needs and circumstances. Meditate on the truths you want to take hold in their lives by the power of the Spirit of God. Celebrate the reality of God's transforming work in their lives. Consider asking a few trusted friends to pray for them as well, sharing your specific requests as it seems appropriate to do so.

- Integrate the "re-collection" or "centering down" approach (described in Chapter 2 of *Celebration of Discipline* and suggested for practice in the "Celebrating Meditation" section of this workbook), which crosses over between the Disciplines of meditation and prayer, as a regular part of your sessions of prayer.

Start each time of prayer with five to ten minutes of "palms down, palms up" in order to clear away distractions and preoccupations, leaving you focused and ready to listen to God.

Over time, monitor the nature of the concerns and anxieties you present to God during these times. Maintain journal entries that will reveal any shifts in your sensitivity to the persons involved, attitudes toward prayer, anticipation of God's responses, and recognition of divine intervention and transformation.

■ Repeat the practice of "flash prayers" often enough that it begins to characterize your spontaneous response to people and circumstances around you—whether you encounter them personally, indirectly through others' conversations, or by way of print or broadcast media. Practice this instant intercession in a variety of contexts: waiting at a red light; in line at the bank or grocery store; commuting to work; during and after telephone calls; while reading the newspaper, listening to the radio, or watching TV news; chance meetings or encounters. The possibilities are endless.

Use the Scripture passages that follow to inform the content of your flash prayers. Seek greater sensitivity and awareness to the profound spiritual realities underlying the surface tapestry of everyday life. Ask God to bless others with the hidden love and care that prompt your flash prayers.

SCRIPTURE PASSAGES RELEVANT TO THE PRACTICE OF PRAYER

The Bible is filled with references to prayer, the intimate lifeline connecting human spirit with Holy Spirit. Here are a few passages that are rich with insights into the practice of prayer.

■ *Models of intercession:*

- 1 Samuel 2:1–10 and Luke 1:46–55 (praise and thanksgiving for the miraculous work of God in human history)
- Ephesians 1:16–19 (for growth in spiritual depth and wisdom)
- Philippians 1:3–6 (for partners in ministry)
- 1 Thessalonians 1:2–3 (remembrance of fellow believers)

■ *"How-to" passages on prayer:*

- Psalm 62:8 (how to be honest in prayer)
- Psalm 136:1–3, 26 (how to pray)
- Matthew 6:5–14 (how and what to pray)
- John 15:7 (the proper context for expecting answers to prayer)
- Ephesians 6:18 (when and how to pray)
- Philippians 4:4–7 (how to experience joy and peace through prayer)
- Hebrews 4:14–16 (how to approach God in prayer)
- James 1:5–8 (how to approach God in prayer)
- James 4:3 (how not to pray, and an explanation of unanswered prayer)
- 1 John 3:19–24 (how to be confident in prayer)

■ *The results of prayer:*

- Isaiah 30:19–22 (God's responsiveness to us; divine guidance)
- Jeremiah 29:12–13 (God's responsiveness to us)
- Matthew 18:19–20 (what happens when we pray in community)
- 1 John 1:9 (the prayer of confession)

THOUGHTS FOR CONTEMPLATION

Reflect on the following quotations to stimulate and inform your practice of prayer.

> The first and basic act of theological work is *prayer*. . . . But theological work does not merely begin with prayer and is not merely accompanied by it; in its totality it is peculiar and characteristic of theology that it can be performed only in the act of prayer.

KARL BARTH

> One hot July day, with the sun beating down, and my shirt drenched with perspiration, I stooped over my tiny tomato garden and picked a tomato. Prayer was the last thing on my mind. But as I held it in my hands, I was struck by how beautiful and red it was. Suddenly I was overwhelmed with the simple joy of being alive. I wanted to share the moment with God, to lift the tomato up into His face and laugh with delight over it. It even seemed that God, deep within me, was as delighted at this moment as I was. Together at the center.

> For nearly an hour I went right on with my work in the garden. . . . But inside, in a channel just beneath the surface, a stream of communion flowed silently between God and me. I never actually spoke words to God. I was utterly aware of my business in the garden. But I was somehow praying.

SUE MONK KIDD

Prayer is not simply petition, but strenuous petition. It is not just passive surrender but active pleading with God. It involves not only submission to the will of God but seeking to change his will. It consists not merely in reflection on the promises of God but in taking hold of these promises.

DONALD G. BLOESCH

This morning, as I came from the train and prayed for all the people on the street, I felt new energy surge into me. What it does to all of them to receive that instant prayer I may never know. What it does for me is electrical. It drives out fatigue and thrills one with eager power. How curious one's mind feels thus encircling others. Is Jesus like that?

FRANK LAUBACH

REFLECTION POINTS FOR JOURNAL ENTRIES

In addition to any responses you noted in the sections above, you may find the following "reflection points" helpful as a way of chronicling your experiences with the Discipline of prayer.

- *Reflection point:* How is the practice of prayer leading you into a deeper experience of intimacy with God?

- *Reflection point:* What are your greatest struggles or disappointments in prayer?

- *Reflection point:* What has your practice of prayer been teaching you about yourself and your relationships?

- *Reflection point:* What has your practice of prayer been teaching you about God?

- *Reflection point:* Is your experience of prayer giving you the sense that you are involved in "the deepest and highest work of the human spirit"? Why or why not?

- *Reflection point:* In what ways have you experienced prayer as central to all the other Spiritual Disciplines?

- *Reflection point:* Are there any commitments to prayer that you want to make now, which you will carry through the rest of your journey in this workbook and beyond? (If so, enter them in your "Record of Commitments.")

Celebrating Fasting

Fasting reminds us that we are sustained "by
every word that proceeds from the mouth of
God" (Matt. 4:4). Food does not sustain us;
God sustains us.

Celebration of Discipline, p. 55

SUGGESTIONS FOR FURTHER READING OF
CELEBRATION OF DISCIPLINE, Chapter 4

■ Do you think fasting is required for followers of Christ today? Study the section entitled "Is Fasting a Commandment?" to help frame your answer.

■ Review the summary of biblical teachings on fasting presented in Chapter 4. Write down as many possible reasons for fasting as you can find in this discussion. In some cases, you may want to look up the reference mentioned and read the surrounding context.

■ Study the "who's who" list of biblical fasters—those from church history as well as those outside the Judeo-Christian heritage. Why do you think they valued fasting so much? Why does modern society devalue it so much? How do you account for the difference?

■ Describe what you think are the major differences between fasting that is centered on God and fasting that is not centered on God.

SPECIFIC SUGGESTIONS FOR PRACTICING THE DISCIPLINE OF FASTING

As you consider the practice of fasting in coming weeks, recall any fasting you may have done during the first quarter of your journey with *Celebration of Discipline*. Use that experience as a starting point for your planning here. If you did not experiment with fasting and are just starting out, begin slowly. A few small steps, consistently taken, will help you much more than an ambitious but unrealistic jump-start. Remember to review the specific advice offered in Chapter 4.

The following ideas suggest possibilities for methods of fasting as well as the content of your focus during fasts. You may quicken and deepen the lessons, insights, and spiritual benefits of your practice of fasting by keeping journal entries recording and reflecting on your experiences. As you make any commitments to a continuing practice of fasting, record them in your "Record of Commitments" for easy reference.

■ *Suggested methods of fasting:*

- For beginners: as you feel God leading you to do so, try one brief fast, once per week, of two meals' duration—for example, skip lunch and dinner or perhaps you may decide to skip dinner and the following morning's breakfast.
- For those already experienced with fasting: as you seek God's leading, consider possibilities such as two brief fasts per week, during which you focus on a particular purpose of central concern in your life right now; or a whole-day fast once per week; or set aside a period of fasting related to an upcoming event in your life, a need to clarify major life decisions or direction, or a sacred season or holy day.

- General: engage in a partial fast by abstaining from a particular kind of food or beverage (solid foods, foods with a high-sugar content, caffeine, and so on).
- General: plan periodic fasts around opportunities arising naturally out of your activities or routines—during times of personal planning; in preparation for significant events, projects, challenges, or decisions; accompanying schedule changes or seasonal transitions; prior to worship services or gatherings with a local congregation or small group; before meetings with a counselor, adviser, or mentor; surrounding ministry to others. Write down in advance, wherever you keep a calendar or record of plans and appointments, when you will fast, how long, and for what purpose.
- General: fast from some activity unrelated to food as a way of breaking a pattern or desisting from behavior that is in some way compulsive, unhealthy, or problematic. For example, you might feel led to fast from:

  watching TV

  the media (as a gratification of the need for "instant information" about anything and everything; instead, use the time to reflect on what is significant in life, and see if this gives you a clearer perspective on social events)

  any reading that has become a false substitute or a way of avoiding something you need to face

  self-deprecating remarks

  offering an opinion before being asked to do so

  non-medical use of substances

  excessive busyness or overachievement

- Ask a group of people from your community of believers to consider fasting together for a common purpose—whether related to an issue of concern within the group, or to a needy context outside the group that is a focus of ministry or service. Clarify the timing and duration of your fast, and plan to break your fast together with prayer, thanksgiving, and rejoicing.

■ *Suggested content or focus of fasting:*

- Reflect on the truth that our deepest need is for God, not for physical or material gratification.
- In preparation for worship or fellowship, cultivate an expectancy for your time together through personal confession and thanksgiving, intercession for all those leading and participating, and the movement of the Holy Spirit before, during, and after your gathering.
- Seek clarification and purification of your motives in a particular relationship,

commitment, or involvement. Ask God to allow impurities to rise to the surface of your conscious recognition, so you can confess them, purge them, and open your life to the transforming work of the Holy Spirit.

- Seek the fulfillment of Paul's admonition to "let the word of Christ dwell in you richly" (Col. 3:16) by choosing a particular Scripture passage (for possibilities, consult the following list) to dwell on meditatively and prayerfully.
- Identify an overbearing concern or anxiety to release into God's care. Reflect on Isaiah's declaration that the Lord has "borne our griefs and carried our sorrows" (53:4, KJV) as you imagine Christ lifting the burden from your heart and carrying it for you. Pray that God will use your time of fasting to give you a supernatural experience of peace and joy in the midst of difficult realities.
- Seek divine wisdom and discernment for greater understanding of yourself— why you engage in certain patterns of thought and behavior, where your vulnerabilities are, how God can use your strengths and weaknesses to deepen your maturity in Christ.
- Set apart your fast for thanksgiving and praise. Reflect on all the good gifts of God in your life right now, writing them down as they occur to you. Offer prayers and songs of thanks and praise both in your heart and aloud. Allow this gratitude and joy to spill over to others.
- Since fasting is really feasting on God, focus on receiving the life of God into you. Allow the Scripture to nourish you and strengthen you. Let listening prayer sustain you.
- Identify a need in your life, in your community, or in the world that calls for confession and repentance. Spend the time of your fast in contrition for sins, whether personal or communal (2 Chron. 7:13–14, Rom. 3:23); in thanksgiving for God's forgiveness and freedom (Rom. 8:1–2 ff.); in seeking a cleansed and renewed spirit (Ps. 51:10–12).
- Practice a form of prayer or meditation that you have engaged in during your journey through the Spiritual Disciplines, and combine it with fasting to deepen and intensify your communion with God.

SCRIPTURE PASSAGES RELEVANT TO THE PRACTICE OF FASTING

The following Scripture passages comment directly and indirectly on the practice of fasting. Reflect on them to help you center your fasting on God.

- Isaiah 58 reveals God's displeasure with fasting as an empty human ritual of religious performance, divorced from a life-changing relationship of obedience that results in intimacy with God and ethical integrity in our individual and communal relationships.

- Zechariah 7:5–6 addresses the motives and underlying purposes of fasting. (Read the surrounding context, at least 7:1–8:8, for a sense of what God wanted his people to turn away from, and what he wanted to do in their lives.)

- Matthew 4:1–4 records Jesus' profound statement, when the devil challenged him during his fast in the wilderness, regarding the provision of God. See also John 4:31–34. (Note that Jesus combined fasting and solitude as a way of strengthening himself for the coming trial of temptation.)

- Matthew 6:16–18 records Jesus' corrective for religious people who corrupt their spiritual practices by using them as tools for achieving personal pride and social status.

- Acts 13:1–3 cites an instance of group fasting, in combination with other Disciplines, in the context of commission for ministry.

- Galatians 5:13 is a reminder that freedom in Christ is not a license for indulgence, but an opportunity for serving in love.

THOUGHTS FOR CONTEMPLATION

Reflect on the following quotations to stimulate and inform your practice of fasting.

> During fasting, thankfulness grows toward him who has given humanity the possibility of fasting. Fasting opens the entrance to a territory that you have scarcely glimpsed: the expressions of life and all the events around you and within you get a new illumination, the hastening hours a new, wide-eyed and rich purpose. The vigil of groping thought is replaced by a vigil of clarity; troublesome searching is changed to quiet acceptance in gratitude and humility. Seemingly large, perplexing problems open their centres like the ripe calyces of flowers: with prayer, fasting and vigil in unison, we may knock on the door we wish to see opened.
>
> TITO COLLIANDER

> Fasting must be done unto God, even before the eye of the Father who sees in secret. While avoiding the brazen conceit of the Pharisee and the desire to quote the praise of man, we may still act out of selfish motives, for the gratification of personal desires and ambitions, and without the basic motive being the glory of God.
>
> ARTHUR WALLIS

Fasting reveals the things that control us. We cover up what is inside us with food and other good things, but in fasting these things come to the surface. The first truth that was revealed to me in my early experiences in fasting was my lust for good feelings. It is certainly not a bad thing to feel good, but we must be able to bring that feeling to an easy place where it does not control us. So many attitudes strive to control us: anger, pride, fear, hostility, gluttony, avarice. All of these and more will surface as we fast. It is a blessed release to have these things out in the open so that they can be defeated, and we can live with a single eye toward God.

RICHARD J. FOSTER

A fifth and more weighty reason for fasting is that it is a help to prayer; particularly when we set apart larger portions of time for private prayer. Then especially it is that God is often pleased to lift up the souls of his servants above all the things of earth, and sometimes to rapt them up, as it were, into the third heaven. And it is chiefly as it is a help to prayer that it has so frequently been found a means in the hand of God of confirming and increasing . . . seriousness of spirit, earnestness, sensibility, and tenderness of conscience; deadness to the world and consequently the love of God and every holy and heavenly affection.

JOHN WESLEY

REFLECTION POINTS FOR JOURNAL ENTRIES

Use the following "reflection points" to help stimulate your thoughts and recollections about the significance of your experiences with the Discipline of fasting.

- *Reflection point:* How is the practice of fasting leading you into a deeper experience of intimacy with God?

- *Reflection point:* What have you found to be the greatest benefits of fasting?

- *Reflection point:* What have you found to be the greatest difficulties in fasting?

- *Reflection point:* What has your practice of fasting been teaching you about yourself and your relationships?

- *Reflection point:* What has your practice of fasting been teaching you about God?

- *Reflection point:* In what ways does fasting complement or support your practice of other Spiritual Disciplines?

- *Reflection point:* What practices of fasting do you want to continue in the future—in the coming months as well as after you have moved beyond this workbook?

Celebrating Study

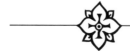

"You will know the truth, and the truth will
make you free" (John 8:32). Good feelings
will not free us. Ecstatic experiences will not
free us. Getting "high on Jesus" will not free
us. Without a knowledge of the truth, we
will not be free.

Celebration of Discipline, p. 63

SUGGESTIONS FOR FURTHER READING OF
CELEBRATION OF DISCIPLINE, Chapter 5

■ How do you think practicing the Discipline of study can help free us from
bondage to fears and anxieties? Cite some specific examples.

■ In your opinion, to what extent do patterns of thought shape behavior, values,
and beliefs?

■   As a way of reviewing the components of study, briefly describe in your own words the nature and benefits of each step: repetition, concentration, comprehension, and reflection.

■   Where do you think the Disciplines of study and meditation overlap?

■   How would you describe the difference between knowledge and wisdom?

■   What do you think are the major distinctions between reading a book and studying a book? Between reading Scripture and studying Scripture?

■   In your experience, how does "live discussion" of what you are reading affect your interaction with the material? Do you seek out others for this kind of discussion? Why or why not?

■   Which "nonverbal books" do you study most often? Which do you desire to pay greater attention to?

SPECIFIC SUGGESTIONS FOR PRACTICING THE DISCIPLINE OF STUDY

Use the following ideas as you find them helpful for practicing the Discipline of study. Check back to your notes in Week 5, and any later weeks, for reviewing your previous practice of study. Start with earlier steps, perhaps seeking counsel from others regarding how to build on accomplishments or address areas of difficulty. To stimulate your thinking, review the advice in Chapter 5 of *Celebration of Discipline*.

Depending upon what form of practice you choose, times and duration and places of study will vary. But common to all these is the need to set apart some block of time—whether a retreat of several days, a weekend out of the month, a full or half-day during the week, or perhaps Sunday afternoons. The components of study require sustained attention to the object of study in order for the Discipline to do its work.

- Select an extended passage, group of chapters, or book from the Bible to study over the next several weeks. Advice from others could be especially helpful here in directing you to portions of Scripture that especially speak to your current needs and interests. For example, if you are struggling with a particular doubt, anxiety, or fear, study the corresponding truth in Scripture that will provide a corrective for the incomplete or distorted understanding you may be laboring under.

  Seek out at least one other person with whom you can discuss the progression of your study. You might also want to consider joining or initiating a small group study of six to eight people who commit to a particular number of meetings over a time frame you all agree on. If you are already part of such a group, apply the following suggestions to the material your group is studying.

  Once you determine what portion of Scripture to study, establish a weekly schedule, perhaps with one or two sessions per week of an hour or more. Between those sessions, you can refer back to your study frequently and briefly: these two modes will complement each other and create a cumulative effect. Gather around you a few Bible study resources—a study Bible with helpful notes in the margin, one or two other translations, a good dictionary, a Bible commentary, a Bible handbook with historical reference material, etc., to aid you in your exploration.

  Structure your time in the study session around the four basic steps of study:

  1. Repetition—read the passage over and over again. Read often enough that you actually begin to memorize much of the material without conscious effort to do so. Pray for openness, clarity, and illumination of mind, heart, and spirit. Come to your study times with a sense of expectancy.
  2. Concentration—pay close attention to detail. Write down everything you observe in the passage. ("Who, what, where, when, why" questions can be helpful here.) Create an outline of the passage, with your own titles for the subsections. Look for major themes, key words, literary style, emotional tone.

3. Comprehension—seek understanding of the foundational meaning(s) of the passage. What truths are communicated? What is the author's primary intent? Synthesize your observations and summarize their significance.

4. Reflection—ask God to reveal what *you* are to learn from this Scripture, how you are to respond to the insights and discoveries of your study, how they are relevant to your understanding of life, of self, of relationships, of God.

■ Choose a book to read and study in coming weeks. Pace yourself appropriately, giving yourself enough time to read slowly and thoughtfully. Schedule a specific number of pages or chapters per week to give yourself a comfortable structure you can follow. To deepen the impact of your study, ask another person or persons to read the same book as well. Schedule meetings with each other— weekly, biweekly, or monthly, for example—during which you share your insights, responses, and questions.

Again, as you study the book, use the four components of repetition, concentration, comprehension, and reflection to structure your approach. Review Chapter 5 of *Celebration of Discipline* to refresh your understanding of these four steps.

The possibilities for what book you study here are endless—"of making many books there is no end" (Eccles. 12:12), in this context a reality for which we can be truly grateful. Consider biographies of those who lived the Christian life deeply and intensely, or of gifted artists, or of great leaders; classics of Christian literature, such as those listed in Chapter 5; evocative poetry (that is accessible to you); quality non-fiction on issues of importance in our world today; finely crafted novels that illuminate the nature and meaning of human existence. It may be preferable to select a book that intrigues or interests you, rather than one you think you *should* read. Enter into your study of books with a sense of joy and freedom—not with the heavy weight of duty and obligation.

■ Study "the book of nature." Choose a spot you can get to easily and quickly. Go there once a week; or once a day if it is within walking distance; or simply as often as you can, however brief the interlude. Write down what you see. Open your senses and heighten your awareness of everything around you. Go at different times of day and notice the changes. Make sketches of what you see, for enjoyment or as an exercise in sharpening your observation. On occasion, take others along, and ask them what they see. Strive to look at things through their eyes. What did they notice that you missed? How did they interpret or respond to the same object in a different way?

Use the four components to help you intensify your study: repeat your observations; concentrate on what is there; comprehend the truths of God revealed in nature; reflect on the significance of the natural world and your ability to take it in.

Keep a journal record of your reflections. Review your entries to monitor how your observations may have shifted or changed. Examine the emotional tone and impact of your reflections. Look for the insights and discoveries that emerge from your study of nature.

■ Under the gaze of God, study people—yourself or others. Consider the following suggestions:

- Study yourself by choosing a particular pattern or relational context, asking God to sensitize you to your own motives, attitudes, moods, and behavior.* Catch yourself in the act of thinking, saying, or doing things that you want to recognize and understand. Through concentration and comprehension, strive for understanding, not judgment. Keep a notebook handy so you can write things down before they slip out of memory.

  In this context, your community of relationships can be especially helpful. Identify a person or persons who know you well and who have earned your trust. Ask them questions such as: "How do I come across in this kind of situation? What are your observations about the way I am responding? What do you think are the key issues I am dealing with in a particular context? What kinds of patterns do you see emerging in how I use my strengths and weaknesses? Where do I need to work on greater honesty with myself, with God, with others? What am I not seeing?" Take notes on their responses, and reflect on them prayerfully.

  Remember to refer all lessons and insights about yourself back to God, ultimately. Do not study yourself in isolation from your relationship with the Spirit who is at work to use these lessons in transforming you according to divine likeness. One of the best ways of maintaining this context for your study of yourself is to share the process of your study with one other person—a spiritual mentor or director, for example, or a close friend. The accountability of this relationship can help keep you on a healthy course that results in positive growth.

---

*Recall here the note of caution from Chapter 5: "This counsel is for reasonably mature and well-adjusted individuals. It is not for mental depressives or others who are bowed low by the burdens of life. For them these exercises are too depressing and self-defeating. If you find your days too heavy for this kind of study, please do not attempt it."

- Study other people, whether loved ones you may live with, acquaintances at work or in your neighborhood, or strangers passing in train stations or airports. Seek a deeper understanding of, and compassion for, your fellow human beings with questions such as: "Why do they act the way they do? What are their hopes, dreams, joys, fears, and hurts? How does God see them? How can I see Christ in them? What draws them forward through life? Where do they find meaning and significance? How do they cope with crisis—personal and global?"

  Keep a notebook with you to record your reflections as they occur to you. Practice really noticing others by drawing brief word pictures of specific individuals—a one-paragraph description capturing what you see in them at the moment. (Don't worry about whether you are guessing accurately—that is not the issue. The issue is how you are developing your attentiveness to others, as well as your understanding of the universal elements of human nature.)

  Use this observation of people to inform your prayer for others—this would integrate particularly well with the practice of "flash prayers," for example. Ask God to deepen your sensitivity to others through this kind of study so that you can intercede for them more effectively.

  Talk about your observations (discreetly and appropriately) with a friend or adviser. Discuss what you are seeing, what you are learning about yourself, what you are learning about people in general.

■ Select an area of art or music to study. This practice can be a deeply enriching and enjoyable experience of study that opens up the visceral dimension as well as the cerebral. Some possibilities:

- Study a particular artist or group of art works—with an art book or at a local gallery or museum. Study the art long enough and often enough so that you begin to see different things each time you come to it. Concentrate on details; try to comprehend the artist's intentions.

  Use the four components to explore such questions as: "What perception of reality is the artist attempting to express? What is the artist communicating about life, about existence, about creativity? What do I like about this art? What do I *not* like about it? How is my life enriched by my ability to view and respond to this art?"

  Show the art to a few friends or acquaintances. Ask for their responses to it, and allow their responses to open up your vision accordingly. Finally, move from asking questions and concentrating on details to experiencing the art itself. What emotions or reactions does it elicit in you? What does this teach you?

- Study music you love or wish to understand in greater depth. Select several pieces by a particular composer, or an extended composition, and listen repeatedly—at least two times a week. Write down your responses to the music each time you listen. What are the emotional nuances you notice? Where are the changes in pace and tone? What are your favorite parts, and why? How does the music make you feel? Is there anything you do not like about it? What pictures, colors, or images does it conjure up?

    If possible, go to live performances of the music you are studying. Consider dipping into literature on the history of the composer, and on how and when the particular pieces were composed—or even how they have been received by various critics in different time periods.

    Use the four components of study to respond to such questions as: "What feelings, emotions, and perceptions of life is the composer expressing? How does the music affect my thoughts and my mood before and after listening to it?"

    Play this music for a few friends or acquaintances. Ask them to respond to it, and let their responses become part of your comprehension of and reflection upon the music.

- Since study is so closely related to meditation, choose an area of meditation you may be practicing—whether on a particular passage of Scripture, a relationship, or an area of personal concern and follow it up with study. Apply the practice of study to give you a wider, more objective framework of understanding. Allow the reflective indwelling of meditation and the conscious analysis of study to feed and enrich each other.

SCRIPTURE PASSAGES RELEVANT TO THE PRACTICE OF STUDY

Reflect on the following Scripture passages to inform and guide your practice of the Discipline of study.

- Psalms 8 models the fruit of studying creation as evidence of God's majesty.

- Ecclesiastes 12:12–13 warns that study for the sake of study is not enough: it must be done in service to deepening our obedience to God.

- Matthew 22:37–40 sums up what God wants of us—including the use of our mind in loving God.

- Luke 18:11 captures the posture of a person whose perpetual self-deception cuts him off from understanding others and the common humanity they share. (Read the surrounding context, 18:9–14, to understand the parable in which this character plays a central role.)

- John 5:39–40 contains a warning about people who study diligently but do not embrace and live according to the truth revealed in what they study.

- John 8:31–32 declares the life-changing fruit of knowing the truth.

- Romans 12:1–2 calls us to offer our whole selves to God by seeking transformation through the renewing of our minds.

- Philippians 4:8 lists the content of what our minds should be dwelling on. (Do not overspiritualize this list. Good and lovely things can be found in many contexts.)

- 2 Timothy 2:15 affirms the importance of knowing the truth well enough to "explain" it rightly.

- 2 Timothy 3:16–17 lists the purposes that the study of Scripture can accomplish in our lives.

THOUGHTS FOR CONTEMPLATION

Reflect on the following quotations to stimulate and inform your practice of study.

One of the reasons why it needs no special education to be a Christian is that Christianity is an education itself. That is why an uneducated believer like Bunyan was able to write a book that has astonished the whole world.

C. S. LEWIS

In prayer, theological work is the inner, spiritual, and vertically directed motion of man; while in study, although similarly external, it runs in a horizontal direction. It is also an intellectual, psychical, and physical, if not fleshly, movement. Theological work can be done only in the indissoluble unity of prayer and study. Prayer without study would be empty. Study without prayer would be blind.

KARL BARTH

To take a book of the Bible, to immerse one's self in it and to be grasped by it, is to have one's life literally revolutionized. This requires study and the training of attention. The student stays with it through barren day after barren day, until at last the meaning is clear, and transformation happens in his life.

ELIZABETH O'CONNOR

A thoroughgoing supernaturalism may be accepted by modern man, not because it provides comfort or emotional satisfaction, but because it makes more sense out of this mysterious world than does any alternative of which we know.

D. ELTON TRUEBLOOD

REFLECTION POINTS FOR JOURNAL ENTRIES

In addition to recording your experiences from any of the questions or practices suggested above, you may find the following "reflection points" helpful as a way of chronicling your journey in spiritual growth through the Discipline of study.

■ *Reflection point:* How is the practice of study leading you into a deeper experience of intimacy with God?

■ *Reflection point:* What do you enjoy most about the practice of study?

■ *Reflection point:* What are your greatest struggles or disappointments in practicing study?

■ *Reflection point:* Does your practice of study lead you into embracing and applying the truth? Or are there some ways in which you allow study to become a substitute for living out the truth?

■ *Reflection point:* What has your practice of study been teaching you about yourself and the world around you?

■ *Reflection point:* What has your practice of study been teaching you about God?

■ *Reflection point:* In what ways, if any, have you found that the practice of study supports or enriches your practice of the other Spiritual Disciplines?

■ *Reflection point:* Which forms of study do you think you are most likely to continue in the future?

Third Quarter: The Outward Disciplines

Reflection and Evaluation

In the third quarter of this workbook, the emphasis shifts from the Inward Disciplines to the Outward Disciplines. This, of course, does not entail simply dropping all involvement with meditation, prayer, fasting, or study. There will most likely be some practice of these Disciplines that you will want to carry into the next twelve weeks. Therefore, during the "Looking Back" section to follow, you will have opportunity to review your experiences from the second quarter to evaluate how you would like to integrate the Inward Disciplines within your primary emphasis on the Outward Disciplines.

Again, as with Week 14, this "hinge week" gives you a chance to stop and reflect on your experiences during the past twelve weeks before moving ahead into the next twelve weeks. Work through the evaluation and planning sections here at a leisurely pace, perhaps over several sessions. If one week isn't enough time, take a few weeks for refreshment and planning.

CELEBRATION

Before you begin the Outward Disciplines, stop to celebrate the insights and joys of your journey thus far and the privilege of anticipating what God has in store for you in the months ahead.

This celebration can take any form: a solitary interlude in a lovely setting for prayer and thanksgiving; time together with a friend over a walk or a meal; an informal gathering of friends for worship and praise. Whatever you decide, take advantage of the opportunity for celebrating a natural point of passage in your travel along the path of spiritual growth.

A NOTE ON APPROACH

The structure of this quarter follows the same approach as does the preceding quarter: an initial week of reflection followed by twelve weeks spread over the four Outward Disciplines, at a suggested pace of three weeks per Discipline. The planning chart will give you opportunity to shift this focus as you desire.

The sections with ideas for practicing the respective Outward Disciplines are again set up with questions for further reading and reflection, specific suggestions for practice, Scripture passages and literary quotations to contemplate, and "reflection points" for journal entries. Although there is room in these sections for you to take notes, plan, and record your experiences, you may also want to use your journal for planning and reflection during the third quarter.

Before you begin the following reflection and evaluation exercises, refresh your perspective once again that practice of the Disciplines is "the path of disciplined grace." If you have begun to treat the Disciplines as performance requirements or to think of them as dull drudgery, take a break from the mechanics of practice for a brief period. Perhaps you have been relying too heavily on willpower and determination—a prescription for fatigue and discouragement.

Remember that the frustration of trying to achieve inner transformation solely through the power of the human can open the door to "a wonderful new realization: inner righteousness is a gift from God to be graciously received. The needed change within is God's work, not ours. The demand is for an inside job, and only God can work from the inside. We cannot attain or earn this righteousness of the kingdom of God; it is a grace that is given."

As you enter a new quarter, let your thoughts dwell on the joyful freedom that is ours when we "place ourselves before God so that he can transform us." Think of your practice as sowing to the Spirit: providing the right conditions for the gracious work of God in producing inner growth. Start this next segment of your journey with a fresh sense of expectancy.

LOOKING BACK

As you are ready to look back at the second quarter, work through the following questions to help you evaluate your experiences. Feel free to skip any questions for which you lack time or interest.

■ How would you describe the high points or deepest satisfactions of your experiences in preceding weeks?

■ How would you describe the chief struggles or frustrations of your experiences in preceding weeks?

■ Which Inward Disciplines were the most enjoyable, and which were the least enjoyable?

■ What were the most important insights you learned about yourself and your relationships?

■ What were the most important insights you learned about God?

■ Check the response that best describes how you are feeling at this point about your journey through the Spiritual Disciplines:

☐ Very positive; eager to move ahead into the next quarter
☐ Generally encouraged, with some concerns for adjusting perspective or practice
☐ Cautious about continuing because of difficulties or discouragement
☐ Overwhelmed and in need of a break
☐ Losing interest in continuing
☐ Not sure

■ Does your response suggest any particular steps you ought to be taking in order to refresh your approach to the journey? For example:

- Reduce expectations for practice—cut back on the number of Disciplines you may be trying to integrate; build in fewer activities on a weekly basis; if your planning is overly ambitious, break it down into smaller and easier steps.
- Identify reasons for discouragement—perhaps you are focusing on results rather than obedience; you may be in need of closer companionship; the Disciplines may seem like laws rather than graces, robbing you of a sense of freedom and joy.
- Stop for a few weeks to allow your responses to settle out—you may need a clean break from focusing on the Disciplines for a few weeks; you might simply need more time with the Inward Disciplines, perhaps on a maintenance level, before moving on.

■ To help you identify and evaluate what responses you are having, talk over how you are feeling with a spiritual companion or group of friends.

LOOKING AHEAD

Based on your evaluations above, work through the following questions to help you consider how to focus your journey through the Outward Disciplines in the next twelve weeks. Answer those questions that seem most helpful to you in gathering your thoughts.

■ What desires and concerns regarding your spiritual growth do you want to address in the weeks ahead?

■ Which Outward Disciplines are you most eager to explore in greater depth in the months ahead?

- Which positive experiences from the past twelve weeks do you want to build on?

- In exploring the Outward Disciplines, what do you want to do differently from your experiences in exploring the Inward Disciplines?

- Look back at your notes and journal entries from Weeks 6 through 9. Are there any specific practices of the Outward Disciplines you experimented with during those weeks that you want to incorporate in the third quarter?

- Take time to review your "Record of Commitments." This exercise will help you identify which goals you want to carry forward from the second quarter into the third quarter. Pray for wisdom and discernment, and seek guidance from others in confirming the directions you choose. This is an important pivot point between major segments of your journey. So treat this step seriously—but not too seriously. Do not worry about taking a wrong step, for in one sense in the presence of God it is not possible to take a wrong step. He will show you if you are running ahead or lagging behind. Thus, chart your course confidently knowing that you are safe in his loving care.
  Consider the following steps:

  1. Cross off any commitments you previously recorded that no longer seem important, valuable, or realistic.
  2. Comb back through your notes and journal reflections from your exploration of the Inward Disciplines. Look for any desires or goals for ongoing practice of meditation, prayer, fasting, or study that you do want to enter in your "Record of Commitments."
  3. Update your "Record of Commitments" accordingly.

PLANNING FOR THE THIRD QUARTER

The suggested structure shown in the following planning chart allows three weeks of focus for each Outward Discipline. Take time now to consider whether you want to follow this structure or create an alternative arrangement. Talk over your reflections with a spiritual mentor, friend, or support group who can help you clarify how God is leading you. If you are exploring these Disciplines in a group context, then make the decision a matter of group discussion and prayer.

After giving the matter careful consideration, map out your path through the Outward Disciplines for the next twelve weeks. Note any changes in the right-hand column of the planning chart. (You might want to pencil in these notations, in case you change plans in coming weeks as experiences and the guidance of the Spirit lead you into new directions.)

Suggested structure	Week	Alternative structure
Simplicity	28	
	29	
	30	
Solitude	31	
	32	
	33	
Submission	34	
	35	
	36	
Service	37	
	38	
	39	

HEADING INTO EACH DISCIPLINE

As you head into sections on Outward Disciplines, take time to get an overall perspective on how you want to focus your practice. As you begin each section, follow these four steps to maximize the benefit of the ideas for in-depth exploration of each Outward Discipline:

1. Read through the ideas listed and familiarize yourself with them. Circle or check those you think you want to use.
2. Refer back to your planning chart to refresh your memory regarding how many weeks you want to spend with this Discipline.
3. Set goals for what you want to do each week, based on the ideas you circled or checked. If you would rather not keep these goals "in your head," write them down in your journal—perhaps assigning weekly pages for the duration of your focus on this Discipline, with the goals as the heading.

    This exercise will establish a helpful target, even if you shift your specific focus during a given week.
4. Review your "Record of Commitments" for your intentions regarding ongoing practice of other Disciplines. If you desire to integrate any goals listed there with your exploration of meditation in coming weeks, make a note of those goals on the appropriate pages in your journal.

Once you have taken these four steps, you will be well prepared to head into each Outward Discipline with at least an initial direction for how you want to proceed.

IDEAS FOR WEEKLY PLANNING

At the start of each week, perhaps on Sunday evenings, spend a half-hour getting perspective on where you are in your journey. Your journal will be an invaluable support for this time by giving you a place to write down your reflections and plans. You might simply mark a new page with "Weekly Planning" and the date, so later on you can go back and find it easily.

Here are a few ideas for how to make good use of this weekly review:

1. Take a mini-break by mentally stepping back from your progress through the Spiritual Disciplines. Pause to thank God for grace for the journey.
2. Reflect on the significance of your experiences in the preceding week (the "reflection points" listed at the end of each in-depth Discipline section are intended for this purpose).
3. Check back to your overall plan for the third quarter, as you sketched it out in the planning chart. If you want to shift the time frames you decided on earlier, change the chart accordingly. Also, check your "Record of Commitments" for practice of other Disciplines you want to carry into the week, writing it down if you find it helpful to do so.
4. Review your responses to the questions you answered in the earlier "Looking Ahead" section. Make note of any desires or commitments you want to carry forward into the coming week. If you have assigned weekly pages and written down goals for practicing the current Discipline, review those goals and adjust them if necessary.
5. Throughout the week, keying off your weekly goals, work through the material you have circled or checked. Proceed at whatever pace is comfortable for you. Space has been provided in the individual in-depth Discipline sections for responses and notes, but you may find it helpful to record key insights or experiences in your journal as they occur during the week.

WRAPPING UP HINGE WEEK 27

In your journal or in the space provided below, note any additional thoughts and reflections from this planning week.

Celebrating Simplicity

Simplicity sets us free to receive the provision
of God as a gift that is not ours to keep and
can be freely shared with others.

Celebration of Discipline, p. 85

SUGGESTIONS FOR FURTHER READING OF
CELEBRATION OF DISCIPLINE, Chapter 6

■   What do you think are the most important elements of the inward reality of
simplicity?

■   What do you think are the most important elements of an outward life-style of
simplicity?

■ Review the Scripture references cited in "The Bible and Simplicity" in Chapter 6. Look up the surrounding contexts for those passages that seem especially important to you. Then summarize what you think are key biblical values regarding material possessions.

■ In your opinion, what are some of the most common distortions or misunderstandings of simplicity (inwardly and outwardly)?

■ How would you describe what it means practically to seek the kingdom of God above all else in life?

■ Would you change or add anything to the list in Chapter 6 of the three inward attitudes of simplicity and the ten controlling principles for an outward expression?

SPECIFIC SUGGESTIONS FOR PRACTICING THE DISCIPLINE OF SIMPLICITY

Refer back to any experiences with the Discipline of simplicity during the first quarter of this workbook, particularly Week 6. Start there as you consider how to focus your efforts in coming weeks. Many of the following suggestions will prove more helpful if you frequently refer back to the practical advice in Chapter 6 of *Celebration of Discipline*. Enter any goals you choose in your "Record of Commitments."

If you are presently part of a group, consider asking group members to try one of the following suggested practices with you. Mutual support, feedback, and encouragement can broaden the lessons you learn and help them take hold in a deep and lasting way.

■ Take a half-day (or longer) retreat to reflect on areas of your life in which you want to concentrate your practice of the Discipline of simplicity. Consider spending time during your retreat in meditation, prayer, and fasting as preparation for your reflection. As you think through where you want to experience simplicity in your life use the following chart to help you identify specific areas of focus.

Area	Clutter I want to clear away	Freedom of simplicity I want to experience

The "Area" column might include: personal growth, spiritual commitments, family life, relationships, work, professional development, health, home management, volunteer commitments, and so forth. In the middle column, list the "clutter" you want to clear away: for example—unnecessary or obsessive concerns with things that are not very significant; anxiety or worry you want to let go of; overburdening expectations, whether self-induced or externally imposed; tasks to which you should be saying no; procrastinating or avoiding important responsibilities; commitments made for the wrong reasons; selfishness; irresponsible use of time or money; status seeking; talking carelessly or out of hidden or manipulative agendas; addictive behavior. In the third column, crystallize your thoughts in a brief picture of what you want to move toward in a given area: freedom from anxiety; an attitude of trust instead of obsessive concern; a generosity of spirit; generosity with resources and material goods; a greater unity of what's important to you and how you live; freedom from living for other people's approval; wisdom and discernment in handling pressures and expectations; plain and honest interaction with others; careful use of resources; strengthening your personal integrity; making conscious choices rather than passively allowing them to be made for you; and more.

After you finish your reflections, spend some time planning for putting these reflections into action. Number the items in priority order. Then assign the top one, or a few of the most important, to upcoming time periods: perhaps one area each month for the next three months, or one major area over the coming year. You can break it down further within those time periods as you set small goals for yourself. Be realistic, and don't take on more plans for change than you will really be willing and able to address. The exercise itself that you go through on this retreat will have a positive impact simply by heightening your awareness.

Finally, close your retreat in prayer and celebration. Ask God to lead you into new patterns of thinking and acting that will help you practice simplicity in the areas you identified. Thank and praise God for the gift of life in Christ, which is what makes it possible for us to experience simplicity.

Groups who take this retreat together might want to follow these steps:

- Open with joint worship and prayer.
- Break up for individual time to fill in the chart.
- Regroup and discuss what kinds of things you put in your charts.
- Break up again to assign priority order to items in your charts.
- Gather again to discuss what you learned from establishing priorities and planning accordingly.
- Close the retreat with group prayer and celebration.

■ Take a personal inventory of where your attitudes coincide with or depart from the inner attitudes of simplicity by responding honestly to the following three groups of questions:

1. "How much of my life do I receive as a gift of God? What parts do I hold onto with the assumption that I have a right to do what I want with them because I worked hard for them and earned or acquired them by my efforts?"

2. "Do I trust everything in my life to God's care and protection? How much time and energy do I spend worrying about what might happen to people, things, or circumstances in my life? What patterns of thought or behavior in my life arise out of an anxious attempt to control the unknown or eliminate uncertainties?"

3. "Am I free to make my possessions and resources available to others? Or do I cling to them in fear that sharing means losing? What am I willing to share, and what am I not willing to share? Where do I exhibit a selfishness that God wants me to let go of?"

Set aside at least two sessions for each of the these three areas. In the first session, pour out your thoughts without stopping to evaluate them. In the second session, go back and evaluate those responses critically, looking for areas in which you were not thorough or scrupulously honest with yourself. Edit your responses appropriately, and summarize the final results in your journal reflections.

When you have spent at least six sessions on this personal inventory, you will have some very helpful material to point you in directions for practicing the Discipline of simplicity in its outward expressions. Seek counsel from a friend, adviser, or support group regarding effective and appropriate ways to work on these areas of need in your life. Incorporate the other Spiritual Disciplines—such as meditation, prayer, fasting, study, confession, celebration—in addressing these inward issues.

■ Spend three weeks or more focusing on what it means to seek the kingdom of God *first*. Ask God to give you a foundational understanding of how this focus should direct your practice of simplicity. Employ the other Disciplines to reflect on how to live out the personal and social righteousness of the kingdom. Ideas here might include:

- Memorize and meditate on a key passage about the kingdom, such as Matthew 6:25–33 (see other Scripture passages listed in the following section).
- Combine prayer and meditation in listening to God for guidance in how to seek God's kingdom above all other concerns.
- Study Scripture passages, commentaries, and topical books on the subject of the kingdom of God.
- Set aside periods of fasting in which you affirm that seeking the kingdom should be our primary focus; food and material necessities will be provided by God and should not occupy our primary attention or concern.
- Practice solitude as a way of quieting the clamor of the everyday concerns Jesus calls us to leave behind in our seeking of the kingdom.

- Look for ways to submit to the authority of the kingdom of God, rather than living as though you are under only your own authority. Surrender body, mind, and spirit to the Lord's purposes, not your own.
- Choose to be a servant in the kingdom of God by countering the natural tendencies of the self to place itself first in importance and priority. "Let each of you look not to your own interests, but to the interests of others" (Phil. 2:4).
- Practice confession—corporately—by acknowledging and repenting of the needs and desires and worries you put ahead of the kingdom of God.
- Seek the kingdom first by acknowledging its primacy with others in worship as you celebrate your common citizenship and affirm your first love. Prepare for and enter into the worship service as a unique opportunity to experience kingdom life with intensity and immediacy. View worship as a ceremony in which you publicly witness to your identity as one who seeks the kingdom of God first.
- Practice guidance in seeking divine insight, mediated through others, regarding areas in which you can grow in seeking the kingdom above the distractions and preoccupations of living.
- Celebrate the good news of the kingdom that Jesus announced: the kingdom is already here, by the power of the Spirit of God, and yet it is still to come, as we wait for the final return of Jesus Christ. Whether you are alone, in spontaneous fellowship with one or two others, or in the gathering of a believing community, celebrate the reality that we are privileged to live in now and the glorious hope that awaits us.

Groups may want to select a few of these ideas to work on together, and meet occasionally to practice or discuss them.

■ Choose one of the ten controlling principles listed in Chapter 6 to guide you in the outward expression of simplicity. These are presented so specifically and practically that they furnish numerous suggested action plans for practicing simplicity.

One approach would be to choose three of these principles to focus on for the next three weeks. Each week, take at least one specific step or perform one particular act as a way of expressing simplicity in that area.

Another approach might be to choose one principle that is most relevant to your life right now. Write it down on a card you can take with you, and set it out before you for frequent review. Decide that you will take at least one step each week (you will probably end up taking many more, but this commitment will anchor your decision and keep you moving), over whatever time period you establish, to express this outward reality.

A third possibility is to select one idea as a group project. For example, weed out possessions and pool them in a community garage sale. Use the money for something the group decides is important—supporting a local outreach, meeting a financial need for an individual or family, beautifying the neighborhood.

However you seek to put these principles into action, remember that you must be cultivating the inward reality at the same time—otherwise your efforts risk being simply a form of behavior modification. For each principle, review what you feel to be the necessary inner attitudes and orientation, and seek divine renewal of your heart and mind in these areas. In particular, if you are giving to others you will want to do so expecting nothing in return. Only in this way can your gift be a blessing rather than a curse.

SCRIPTURE PASSAGES RELEVANT TO THE PRACTICE OF SIMPLICITY

The following Scripture passages have much to teach us about the practice of simplicity. (These and many others are cited in Chapter 6.) Reflect on them to help guide you in cultivating the inward reality and outward expression of this Discipline.

- Psalm 62, which is a profound expression of trust in God, declares the insubstantial nature of earthly life and goods.

- Psalm 78 records the Israelites' failure to trust God for their needs, despite his miraculous intervention. (See especially verses 18–22.)

- Matthew 6:25–33 reveals the foundational orientation in life that undergirds the Discipline of simplicity. (See also Luke 12:13–34.)

- Matthew 13:44–46 contains two brief parables teaching that the kingdom is to be cherished above all earthly possessions.

- Luke 10:38–42 records Jesus' affirmation of what is most important in life, above the worries and distractions of daily living.

- Acts 2:44–45 provides a glimpse of the freedom and generosity that characterized the life-style of believers in the early church.

- Philippians 4:11–13 addresses the issue of freedom from anxiety regarding the nature of our circumstances.

THOUGHTS FOR CONTEMPLATION

Reflect on the following quotations to stimulate and inform your practice of simplicity.

O God, we beseech thee to save us this day from the distractions of vanity and the false lure of inordinate desires. Grant us the grace of a quiet and humble mind, and may we learn of Jesus to be meek and lowly of heart. May we not join the throng of those who seek after things that never satisfy and who draw others after them in the fever of covetousness. Save us from adding our influence to the drag of temptation. If the fierce tide of greed beats against the breakwaters of our soul, may we rest at peace in thy higher contentment. In the press of life may we pass from duty to duty in tranquillity of heart and spread thy quietness to all who come near.

WALTER RAUSCHENBUSCH

I have said that Abraham possessed nothing. Yet was not this poor man rich? Everything he had owned before was his still to enjoy: sheep, camels, herds, and goods of every sort. He had also his wife and his friends, and best of all he has his son Isaac safe by his side. He had everything, *but he possessed nothing.* There is the spiritual secret. There is the sweet theology of the heart which can be learned only in the school of renunciation.

A. W. TOZER

. . . Christian simplicity must at all times be dialectical. And if its practitioner is to be *in* the world even while *not of* it, he must find the way to differ from the world without telling it to go to hell at the same time.

VERNARD ELLER

It is crucial that we deal with economics from a Christian perspective because this question has been for the most part ignored. The predominant ethic is strict individualism in regard to wealth. What Christians do with their wealth has been considered their private business. The church, friends, and even the Christian faith are expected to keep out of this area. It is a subject one does not discuss with friends. Complete secrecy shrouds our private economic life. We tend to be even more sensitive about our economic life than our sex life.

ARTHUR G. GISH

REFLECTION POINTS FOR JOURNAL ENTRIES

Use the following "reflection points" as you find them helpful to explore the progress and significance of your experiences in practicing the Discipline of simplicity.

- *Reflection point:* How is the practice of simplicity leading you into a deeper experience of intimacy with God?

- *Reflection point:* In what ways, if any, has the Discipline of simplicity opened up new areas of freedom in your life?

- *Reflection point:* What frustrations, if any, have you encountered in practicing the Discipline of simplicity?

- *Reflection point:* What has your practice of simplicity been teaching you about yourself and your relationships?

- *Reflection point:* What has your practice of simplicity been teaching you about God?

- *Reflection point:* How does your practice of simplicity relate to your practice of the other Spiritual Disciplines?

- *Reflection point:* What practices of simplicity do you want to integrate in your life on a long-term basis? Are there any specific commitments that you want to make for coming weeks and months?

Celebrating Solitude

Don't you feel a tug, a yearning to sink
down into the silence and solitude of God?
Don't you long for something more? Doesn't
every breath crave a deeper, fuller exposure
to his Presence? It is the Discipline of
solitude that will open the door.

Celebration of Discipline, pp. 108–9

SUGGESTIONS FOR FURTHER READING OF
CELEBRATION OF DISCIPLINE, Chapter 7

■   Review the Scripture passages cited in Chapter 7 that record times when Jesus withdrew to be alone. What aspects of Jesus' inward "heart solitude" do you want to cultivate in your life, and why?

■   How would you describe the relationship between silence and solitude? (In what ways do they interrelate, intensify, and complete one another?)

■ When, if at all, have you ever experienced silence as helplessness? When, if at all, have you experienced silence as freedom from the need to explain or justify yourself?

■ What counsel would you give a person who is going through an experience of "the dark night of the soul"?

■ In what ways have you experienced solitude as an opening door into a deeper encounter with the Presence of God?

SPECIFIC SUGGESTIONS FOR PRACTICING THE DISCIPLINE OF SOLITUDE

Review your notes from Week 7 regarding your practice of the Discipline of solitude. Build on any experiences you have had so far as you consider the following suggestions.

Remember that solitude is not simply "being alone." Learn to practice it in the midst of people as well as away from people. Draw on your relationships with others as you seek the fruit of solitude: an increased sensitivity to others and a new freedom to be with people.

■ To counteract the pull of demands and pressures in your life, take advantage of the "little solitudes" in your daily routines for reorienting your perspective. Consider using these times of inward quietness for: rest and refreshment; a checkpoint for evaluating whether you are making conscious choices about how you spend your day or drifting with the current of external forces; an interlude of communion with God; listening for the divine Whisper of guidance for your day.

■ Practice the Discipline of solitude in combination with one of the other Spiritual Disciplines. For example:

- Spend "little solitudes" in some form of intercession, such as flash prayers.
- Set aside weekly sessions in a quiet place to practice "centering prayer" as a way of releasing anxieties and concerns.
- Meditate during regular walks in your neighborhood or a nearby park. Turn them into special times of communion with God, pursuing what Thomas à Kempis calls "a familiar friendship with Jesus."
- Spend time alone to study areas of your life in which silence is an unhealthy practice. They might include, for example, fear of speaking up on justice issues; intimidation by those in position, authority, or particular social status; anxiety regarding the effects of confrontation; and more. Contrast these with your healthy practices of silence to gain better self-understanding.
- Use periods of solitude to engage in re-creating through some form of plea-surable study or celebration (for example, enjoyment of life's good things)— reading, nature watching, sketching, creative writing or journaling, singing or playing an instrument, physical workouts, and so forth.

■ If you are struggling with control of the tongue, spend part or all of one day each week without words. While you refrain from speech, reflect on why this area is difficult for you. For example:

- "I jump in unnecessarily to explain or justify myself because I am afraid of what other people are thinking about me."
- "I engage in religious talk as a way of trying to cover up doubt and convince myself that I believe all of it."
- "Rather than being genuinely myself in speech, I say things in order to win other people's approval or present a particular image I think they want to see." Or, "Rather than being genuinely myself in speech, I refrain from say-ing things because I fear the loss of other people's approval."
- "I tend to say things I don't really mean because I don't stop to think carefully about what I say."
- "I am impulsive in speech because I assume that I won't get the chance to say something unless I take the initiative."
- "I talk compulsively with others as a way of alleviating the discomfort I feel with them, overcoming my uneasiness with silences in conversation, or sub-duing my anxiety over what they might say if I really invited them to tell me."
- "I say things at the wrong time or in the wrong way because I have trouble controlling my feelings."

- "I withdraw from conversation because I think others are not really interested in what I have to say."

As a positive focus during these periods of silence, let your thoughts dwell on cultivating what John Woolman calls "the pure spirit which inwardly moves upon the heart." Ask God to develop this pure spirit within you, so that your words might be "few and full."

■ Consider taking a silent retreat away from home for a day. Make solitude your only purpose. Seek to be drawn into the recreating stillness of the Divine Presence. The following ideas are possible ways to focus your time in retreat:

- Seek the recreating stillness of silent communion with God. Orient your mind and heart in wordless prayer and meditation. Shed the clutter and clatter of everyday living in order to return to your routines cleansed and refreshed. Although you should enter into this silence without imposing goals or objectives on it, you might reflect on the possible fruit of practicing this Discipline in retreat, such as: a renewed clarity in your daily routines, a more genuine use of speech (or refrainment from it), a more thorough self-awareness, a deeper sensitivity to others, a greater inward attentiveness to what is important in life.
- Pursue God's leading for reorienting your life goals. (See the specific instructions in Chapter 7: first edition, pp. 94-95; revised edition, pp. 107–8.)
- If you are undergoing a period of darkness, enter into the deep, inner, listening silence that will lead you to accept rather than fight the dryness, confusion, lostness, or loneliness you may be suffering. Seek openness to God's purposes in this experience rather than release from it.

■ Practice meditation and contemplative prayer, perhaps along with fasting, using devotional literature such as that of St. John of the Cross. Reflect on key Scriptures. For example:

- Psalm 88, an impassioned cry of despair to God
- Isaiah 42:16–17 and 50:10–11, specific references to the experience of darkness
- Lamentations 3:1–33, an affirmation of hope amid unrelenting suffering

■ Practice the Discipline of solitude with others—a close friend or friends, family members, a spiritual mentor, or a small group—by establishing times and places for at least two or three interludes of silence together, for whatever duration on which you collectively agree. Identify a purpose for these silences together, such as:

- Acknowledging that each of you is an individual before God in order to form a genuine community of persons.
- Emphasizing that simple presence is as important as dialogue together.
- Eliminating the distractions of conversational buzz by becoming genuinely aware of each other.
- Opening up your self to wordless forms of communication such as eye contact and touch.
- Listening together to the divine Whisper for guidance on some issue of common concern.

Be creative about times and places—they can be as varied as holding hands in a circle in a softly lit room, walking a trail on a beautiful day, eating a meal together, praying or meditating in intercession or worship, listening to devotional music, riding in a vehicle on a long trip, attending a silent retreat.

SCRIPTURE PASSAGES RELEVANT TO THE PRACTICE OF SOLITUDE

The Scriptures have much to say about the state of mind and heart called solitude. The following passages contain insights into our need for silence, and the importance of being alone with God in the midst of our community with each other.

- Psalm 23, a lyrical meditation on the gracious provision of God, comments on the spiritual refreshment God gives us in quietness (see especially verses 1–3).
- Ecclesiastes 5:1–2 contrasts rash speech with reverent silence.
- Isaiah 30:15 declares the profound importance of rest and quietness.
- Zephaniah 3:17 identifies the nature of the inner fulfillment that may be found in solitude.
- The Gospels cite many instances in which Jesus taught or practiced solitude:
  - in response to tragic news—Matthew 14:12–13.
  - in order to pray—Matthew 14:23, Luke 5:16.
  - in company with his closest companions—Matthew 26:36–46.
  - amid the demands of ministry—Mark 1:32–39.
  - in counseling his disciples to rest from the demands of ministry—Mark 6:30–32.
  - in seeking guidance for making major decisions—Luke 6:12–13.
  - to elude the crowd's attempts to control the events of his life—John 6:15.
- James 3:1–12 discusses the roots, the manifestations, and the effects of our speech.

THOUGHTS FOR CONTEMPLATION

Reflect on the following quotations to stimulate and inform your practice of solitude.

[Do] you now live so that you are conscious of being an individual and thereby that you are conscious of your eternal responsibility before God? Do you live in such a way that this consciousness is able to secure the time and quiet and liberty of action to penetrate every relation of your life? This does not demand that you withdraw from life, from an honorable calling, from a happy domestic life. On the contrary, it is precisely that consciousness which will sustain and clarify and illuminate what you are to do in the relations of life.

SØREN KIERKEGAARD

Under a sense of the divine nearness, the soul, feeling how self is always ready to assert itself, and intrude even into the holiest of all with its thoughts and efforts, yields itself in a quiet act of self-surrender to the teaching and working of the divine Spirit. It is still and waits in holy silence, until all is calm and ready to receive the revelation of the divine will and presence. Its reading and prayer then indeed become a waiting on God with ear and heart opened and purged to receive fully only what He says.
. . . In these [seasons of meditation and waiting on God] a habit of soul must be cultivated, in which the believer goes out into the world and its distractions, the peace of God, that passeth all understanding, keeping the heart and mind. . . . May each one of us learn every day to say, "Truly my soul is silent unto God." And may every feeling of the difficulty of attaining this only lead us simply to look and to trust to Him whose presence makes even the storm a calm.

ANDREW MURRAY

Deserts, silence, solitudes are *not necessarily places but states of mind and heart.* These deserts can be found in the midst of the city, and in the every day of our lives. We need only to look for them and realize our tremendous need for them. They will be small solitudes, little deserts, tiny pools of silence, but the experience they will bring, if we are disposed to enter them, may be as exultant and as holy as all the deserts of the world, even the one God himself entered. For it is God who makes solitude, deserts, and silences holy.

CATHERINE DE HUECK DOHERTY

We would, however, encounter one phenomenon during our climb, a certain kind of loneliness. The further up the mountain we travel, the fewer companions we have. There comes a time when all things seem to drop behind and we find ourselves alone. When we finally arrive on the top, the loneliness is gone for we see things very differently. We see all our former companions and possessions as they really are with no illusions, no regrets, and no attachments. In this rare air of God's love we possess Wisdom, which is the Word of God—Jesus. We see things as he sees them because the breath of his Spirit fills our souls to overflowing.

MOTHER ANGELICA

REFLECTION POINTS FOR JOURNAL ENTRIES

Use the following "reflection points" as you find them helpful for exploring your experiences in practicing solitude.

- *Reflection point:* How is the practice of solitude leading you into a deeper experience of intimacy with God?

- *Reflection point:* In what ways do you experience silence as emptiness? In what ways do you experience silence as richness?

- *Reflection point:* What insights, if any, have you gained into both the freedom of being alone and the freedom of being with others?

- *Reflection point:* What frustrations, if any, have you encountered in practicing the Discipline of solitude?

- *Reflection point:* What has your practice of solitude been teaching you about yourself and your relationships?

- *Reflection point:* What has your practice of solitude been teaching you about God?

- *Reflection point:* In what ways, if any, has your practice of solitude supported or complemented your practice of other Spiritual Disciplines?

- *Reflection point:* What forms of practicing solitude do you want to continue in the months ahead?

Celebrating Submission

> In submission we are at last free to value
> other people. Their dreams and plans become
> important to us. We have entered into a new,
> wonderful, glorious freedom—the freedom to
> give up our own rights for the good of
> others. For the first time we can love people
> unconditionally. We have given up the right
> to demand that they return our love.
>
> *Celebration of Discipline,* p. 112

SUGGESTIONS FOR FURTHER READING OF
CELEBRATION OF DISCIPLINE, Chapter 8

■ Review the opening discussion in Chapter 8, which reminds us that the Disciplines are means to freedom—not ends in themselves. What are some ways in which the Discipline of submission is distorted by this confusion of focus?

■ How can self-denial lead us into discovering our true self—the identity God has given us?

■ Can you identify from personal experience with "the freedom to give up our own rights for the good of others"?

■ Foster uses John Howard Yoder's term *revolutionary subordination* to describe the submission that Jesus taught and lived out. What do you think is "revolutionary" about the submission to which Christians are called?

■ Based on the teaching in Chapter 8, how would you define the practice of submission?

SPECIFIC SUGGESTIONS FOR PRACTICING THE DISCIPLINE OF SUBMISSION

Be sure to review your responses to the questions and suggestions in Week 8. If you have not "experimented" with practicing submission, start with the ideas for practice listed there.

Remember that submission is not something we grit our teeth and force ourselves to do: that would be a violation of the Discipline by turning it into law. Instead, we are called to practice submission voluntarily and freely. This freedom is at the heart of submission, as it is at the heart of all the Disciplines.

Focus on this liberation, the result of obedience, as you consider the following suggestions:

■ Submit yourself to God by performing acts of unconditional love for others. Ask God to show you ways in which you can submit to their interests without expecting anything from them in return. (Pray for wisdom and sensitivity in discerning the limits of submission and acting out of a true spirit of grace. If you sense that you must refuse rather than submit or that your acts arise out of the wrong spirit, stop and seek guidance from a trusted friend or spiritual mentor.) For example:

- If someone asks you to do something that is usually someone else's responsibility, do it cheerfully.
- If you find yourself in disagreement over something that is not a genuine issue of concern, yield to the other point of view.
- If you are criticized unfairly, resist the impulse to defend yourself.
- If a friend or family member wants you to do something you don't feel like doing, do it anyway, freely and graciously.

■ Study your relationships for any evidences of self-pity: the "poor me!" martyrdom syndrome. Ask God to reveal to you where you are still holding onto the need to have things go your way. As you identify and confess this need, seek the freedom to give way to others in genuine and unconditional love.

■ Review the seven areas in which Foster suggests we are to practice submission: to the Triune God, to the Scripture, to our family, to our neighbors and acquaintances, to the believing community, to the helpless and outcast of our society, and to the world as international community. Choose one of these areas in which to focus your practice of submission. Other Disciplines can be helpful here. For example:

- Spend ten to fifteen minutes each morning in listening prayer as you submit the coming day to God's purposes.
- Submit yourself to the Scripture by hearing it preached in worship. Then reflect on the same text in your own sessions of meditative reading and study. Make it your goal to hear, receive, and obey the Word.
- Submit to the interests of others in your family community by taking time to listen carefully to family members.
- Look for small, hidden acts of service you can perform for neighbors and acquaintances.
- Volunteer for a task in your community of faith. Submit to the needs of the group without looking for recognition or position.

- Submit to the needs of the abandoned and helpless persons in society. Whether in intercession or direct service, look for ways to sacrifice your own interests in identification with them.
- Choose a way to participate responsibly in meeting global needs. Seek God's leading for how you should practice submission as a member of the world community.

■ Examine the nature of your relationships to human authority, and distinguish where revolutionary subordination commands you to live in submission to that human authority, and where it commands you to resist submission because that authority has become destructive. For example, you might choose a relationship from any of the following contexts:

- immediate family
- private organization or association, of which you are a member
- educational or religious institution
- employer or work supervisor
- colleagues or committee structure
- local, state, or national government
- support group or individual sponsor
- counselor or doctor
- spiritual adviser or mentor
- local body of believers

If you conclude that you are practicing a form of submission that is distorted or destructive, get help from a reliable source as you seek the guidance of the Holy Spirit for the proper response.

■ Reflect on where in your life you find it difficult to submit to God. Ask God to reveal to you how you might be resisting the work of the Spirit in your life, and why. Use the other Disciplines—meditation, prayer, solitude, confession, guidance—to help guide and structure your reflection.

This could be difficult to do alone. Consider asking another person to do the same thing and then meet regularly to discuss and monitor your respective experiences. If you are part of a group, ask the others to consider spending a session on this issue. Additionally, consult a close friend or spiritual mentor for help in keeping you honest before God and accountable to address needs for change.

SCRIPTURE PASSAGES RELEVANT TO THE PRACTICE
OF SUBMISSION

The following passages specifically address the practice of submission. Reflect on them prayerfully and in consultation with others to learn how they should guide and inform your voluntary subjection to the way of the cross.

- Genesis 50:15–21 records the reconciliation of Joseph with his brothers, who had grievously wronged him many years before. Joseph's response models the godly submission that characterized his entire life. (For the origin of the conflict, see Genesis 37 ff.)

- Psalm 32:8–9 emphasizes the importance of voluntary submission to God's instruction and guidance.

- Mark 8:34–35 (see also Luke 9:23–24) records Jesus' foundational teaching on self-denial—which, paradoxically, is the way to self-discovery.

- Ephesians 5:21 contains the key instruction for mutual subordination out of reverence for Christ that is the foundation for submission within family life.

- Philippians 2:3–9 presents Jesus' life of servanthood and death on the cross as the model for our way of living with each other.

- 1 Peter 2:13–25 places submission to human authority in the larger context of our calling to follow the example of Christ's submission. (See also Romans 13:1–7.)

THOUGHTS FOR CONTEMPLATION

Reflect on the following quotations to stimulate and inform your practice of submission.

> How desperately we need to see that mutual submission in marriage and the family is not subtraction of wifely submission, but the addition of husbandly submission. Only that is the perfect biblical equation. In decision making within marriage, the "one" who makes the decisions should be the "two become one."

GRETCHEN GAEBELEIN HULL

Jesus:
My dear friend, abandon yourself, and you will find me. Give up your will and every title to yourself, and you will always come out ahead, for greater grace will be yours the moment you turn yourself over to me once and for all.
Disciple:
Lord, how often shall I resign myself, and in what ways am I to abandon myself?
Jesus:
Do so always and at all times, in small things as in great.

THOMAS À KEMPIS

The frail person is raised up and God withdraws himself from the mighty. Compassionate, he lowers himself and descends to the one who needs him. Therefore, frequently submit yourself that you may always be raised up by him.

MARIE ANNE MAJESKI

. . . mutual submission is much more than an ethical novelty or a convenient solution to the war of the sexes. Mutual submission pertains to the very nature of Christ and His ministry. It reaches deeply into the creation work of God. It provides the archetypal paradigm of God's dealings with mankind through Christ.

GILBERT BILEZIKIAN

REFLECTION POINTS FOR JOURNAL ENTRIES

Use the following "reflection points" as you find them helpful for exploring your experience with the Discipline of submission.

- *Reflection point:* How is the practice of submission leading you into a deeper experience of intimacy with God?

- *Reflection point:* What experiences of submission, if any, have brought you a sense of joy and freedom?

- *Reflection point:* In what areas of your life do you find it most difficult to practice submission, and why?

- *Reflection point:* What has your practice of submission been teaching you about yourself and your relationships?

- *Reflection point:* What has your practice of submission been teaching you about God?

- *Reflection point:* In what ways, if any, has your practice of submission been guided or supported by other Spiritual Disciplines?

- *Reflection point:* In what areas do you especially desire God's guidance and grace for practicing submission?

Celebrating Service

> True service builds community. It quietly and
> unpretentiously goes about caring for the
> needs of others. It draws, binds, heals,
> builds.
>
> *Celebration of Discipline,* p. 129–30

SUGGESTIONS FOR FURTHER READING OF
CELEBRATION OF DISCIPLINE, Chapter 9

■ When are you most aware, if ever, of your need to cultivate the Christian virtue
of humility?

■ Do you find Foster's distinction between "choosing to serve" and "choosing to
be a servant" helpful? Why or why not?

■   What do you think is joyous about voluntary servitude?

■   How would you describe the difference between "mastering the mechanics of service" and "experiencing the Discipline"?

■   How would you describe the difference between *acting* like a servant and *being* a servant?

SPECIFIC SUGGESTIONS FOR PRACTICING THE DISCIPLINE OF SERVICE

Use the following suggestions as you find them helpful for practicing service, and refer back to the practical advice in Chapter 9 of *Celebration of Discipline.* Build on any experiences you may have begun in Week 9 or in other weeks during the first quarter.

Remember that service, like submission, is to be undertaken voluntarily and joyfully. Let this anticipation of freedom guide your attitudes and expectations as you explore the way of servanthood. (As you desire to do so, record any goals in your "Record of Commitments" as a handy reference.)

■   Identify an area in which you may be practicing a form of "self-righteous service." Seek to replace it with true service. For example, ask yourself:

- "Am I serving in the frantic energy of human effort, or am I serving in sensitivity to God's promptings?"
- "Do I wait for opportunities that seem important enough to merit my service, or am I willing to act on any and all opportunities that come my way?"
- "Am I focused on the approval of people, or on the approval of God?"
- "Do I judge the value of my serving based on outcome, or do I take delight simply in the serving?"

- "Do I make judgments about whether someone is worthy of my service, or do I view myself as the servant of all, regardless of their status, position, or receptivity to me?"
- "Do I serve only when I feel like it, or am I faithful to continuing serving regardless of my feelings?"
- "Do I view servanthood as a role to take on and put off, or do I accept it as a permanent life-style?"
- "Do I insist upon serving others according to what I think they need, or do I listen and wait without forcing opportunities to help?"
- "Is my service focused on building community or glorifying my individual role in it?"

You may want to identify one particular area or pattern from the above list in which to concentrate your pursuit of true service. Study your attitudes and behavior as you pray for the inward transformation that will enable you to participate freely in what Foster calls "the ministry of the towel."

■ Look for ways to serve in hiddenness. Catch yourself in the act of looking for recognition. Seek the joy of promoting the welfare of others in ways seen by God alone. Support your practice of this service with the other Disciplines; for example:

- Practice listening prayer in asking God to reveal to you opportunities for hidden service.
- Confess to a companion of faith those areas in which "the desires of the flesh" have hindered you from true service.
- Study those you have opportunity to serve in order to follow William Law's counsel to "condescend to all the weaknesses and infirmities of your fellow-creatures, cover their frailties, love their excellencies, encourage their virtues, relieve their wants, rejoice in their prosperities, compassionate their distress, receive their friendship, overlook their unkindness, forgive their malice. . . ."
- Take time in solitary meditation to reflect on how your acts of hidden service are affecting your attitude toward service, your awareness of the Presence of God, and how you see yourself in relationship with others.

■ Choose one of the following areas (from Chapter 9) for focusing your practice of service. Over a period of several weeks, ask God to deepen your sensitivity to others and increase your awareness of opportunities to serve others in this way.

- Help others with the service of small things.
- Support and protect the reputation of others.
- Accept the service of others graciously and gratefully.

- Look for ways to be courteous by acknowledging others, treating them kindly, and affirming their worth.
- Offer the service of hospitality—however brief the time together—to a friend, neighbor, colleague, or acquaintance in need of human attention or friendship.
- Develop an inner orientation of listening to others—and through them, to God. Hone your listening skills: remain quiet and speak only when appropriate; maintain eye contact along with presence of mind and heart; communicate personal warmth, interest, and trustworthiness; suspend personal thoughts and concerns to dwell on the importance of the other person's thoughts and concerns.
- Look for an opportunity to bear another's burdens this week—for example, help . . . a child who is experiencing some personal disappointment . . . a friend or loved one whose anxieties could be lightened by your attentive care . . . a lonely individual who needs a visit . . . a needy person who could use a helping hand . . . someone in the grieving process who could be helped by a small act of kindness. . . .
- In prayerful sensitivity to the guidance of the Spirit, share with another person some spiritual insight or reflection—the "word of Life"—God has given to you that you feel led to express.

SCRIPTURE PASSAGES RELEVANT TO THE PRACTICE OF SERVICE

Reflect on the following Scripture passages to motivate and guide you in developing a servant life-style.

- Joshua 24:14–27, a record of Joshua's challenge to the people of Israel to renew their covenant with God, provides insight into the all-or-nothing commitment to servanthood which God asks of us.

- Isaiah 52:13–53:12 describes the ministry of God's suffering servant, the Messiah of Israel. (See also Isaiah 42:1–9, 49:1–7, and 50:4–9.)

- Jesus' teaching in Matthew 20:25–28 and Mark 9:33–35 reverses the world's value system in the priority it places on service.

- John 13:1–20 recounts Jesus' dramatic teaching of servanthood as he washed the disciples' feet and set an example for all believers.

■ 1 Corinthians 12:1–11 affirms the legitimacy of the service that each of us is equipped by the power of the Spirit to offer. Paul emphasizes that the purpose of these gifts is for serving the common good, not for gaining individual advantage or status.

■ Ephesians 6:5–9 and Colossians 3:22–25 define the inner nature of servanthood amid the external realities of unjust treatment.

THOUGHTS FOR CONTEMPLATION

Reflect on the following quotations to stimulate and inform your practice of service.

. . . Jesus calls us to downward mobility—to the seats at the bottom. His disciples defer to others. They happily yield up the good seats. In fact, they are so busy waiting on tables that they don't have time to sit. Serving is their occupation, not seat picking.

DONALD KRAYBILL

. . . service is a willing, working, and doing in which a person acts not according to his own purposes or plans but with a view to the purpose of another person and according to the need, disposition, and direction of others. It is an act whose freedom is limited and determined by the other's freedom, an act whose glory becomes increasingly greater to the extent that the doer is not concerned about his own glory but about the glory of the other.

KARL BARTH

It is possible to be religious, in the sense of having the assurance of personal salvation, and yet be blind or insensitive to vast areas of human suffering. While it is true that life is never adequate without reverence, it is true, at the same time, that no experience is valid unless it leads to acts of justice and mercy. . . . Christians are asked to combine the basin and the towel with the bread and the wine (John 13:3–17).

D. ELTON TRUEBLOOD

Accepting Christ's call to servanthood means giving up any rights to being in a privileged position in our spiritual warfare or to being protected from that spiritual warfare. Service as Christ's ambassadors will mean the sacrifice of giving up our preconceived ideas about how we and others can best be deployed.

GRETCHEN GAEBELEIN HULL

REFLECTION POINTS FOR JOURNAL ENTRIES

Use the following "reflection points" as you find them helpful for exploring your experience with the Discipline of service.

- *Reflection point:* How is the practice of service leading you into a deeper experience of intimacy with God?

- *Reflection point:* What experiences of service, if any, have brought you joy?

- *Reflection point:* In what areas of your life is it most difficult for you to choose to be a servant, and why?

- *Reflection point:* What has your practice of service been teaching you about yourself and your relationships?

- *Reflection point:* What has your practice of service been teaching you about God?

- *Reflection point:* In what ways, if any, has your practice of service been illuminated or strengthened by other Spiritual Disciplines?

- *Reflection point:* In what areas do you especially desire God's guidance and grace for practicing service?

Fourth Quarter:
The Corporate
Disciplines

Reflection and Evaluation

The fourth and final quarter of this workbook invites in-depth exploration of the Corporate Disciplines. By definition, these Disciplines are practiced through the bonds of community relationships. If you are well established in those relationships, then you can look forward to rich experiences that will build on previous Disciplines. If your journey has tended to be a solo voyage, then the next three months may open up to you the freedom and joy of life with others in a way that will increasingly draw you into the flow of common life in Christ.

Again, the shift in emphasis to the Corporate Disciplines does not mean that you will drop the Inward and Outward Disciplines. In fact, you will find that the Corporate Disciplines are interwoven with and in many ways dependent upon meditation, prayer, fasting, study, simplicity, solitude, submission, and service. The longer you spend with the Spiritual Disciplines, the more their integration will become a natural part of your practice.

Most of the specific ideas for practicing the Corporate Disciplines will suggest integration with the other Disciplines, so don't be too concerned in this quarter about setting specific goals for addressing the other Disciplines directly. Therefore, be careful not to construct an unwieldy or overly ambitious structure of expectations and commitments in this fourth quarter based on the assumption that you must somehow plan to practice all the Disciplines in one form or another.

When the "Looking Back" section prompts you to evaluate what practices of the Inward and Outward Disciplines you want to carry forward into the next few months, be selective. Weed out whatever you feel is unnecessary or overly ambitious. This is not an exercise in time management, nor is it a challenge to personal productivity.

Here again it is important to remember that practice of the Disciplines is concerned with internal reality, not external control. Picture yourself on the path of the spiritual life as described in Chapter 1 of *Celebration of Discipline:* on one side is the heresy of moralism, the way of moral bankruptcy through human strivings; on the other side is the heresy of antinomianism, the way of moral bankruptcy through the absence of human strivings. Your calling is to follow the path of disciplined grace, where you can receive the generous gifts of God and experience the transforming work of grace in Jesus Christ. Remember that "the path does not produce the change; it only places us where the change can occur."

CELEBRATION

Before you begin the Corporate Disciplines, stop to celebrate the events of the journey in the past nine months or more. (If you have stayed with it this far, you will most likely have plenty to celebrate!) Consider writing a prayer, a poem, or a brief summary commemorating the highlights or struggles of your experiences and then read it aloud to several friends.

If you have been using this workbook with a small group, adapt this idea for a special group session. Take turns reading aloud to each other your commemorative reflections. Follow the readings with prayer, singing, a meal together, or time just to relax and play. This meeting can be an enjoyable rite of passage into your final quarter, heightening your anticipation of the rich experiences awaiting you in the months ahead.

A NOTE ON APPROACH

Again, as with Weeks 14 and 27, this "hinge week" gives you a chance to stop and reflect on your experiences during the preceding quarter before moving ahead. Work through the evaluation and planning sections here at a leisurely pace, perhaps over several sessions, taking more than one week if you desire.

The structure of this quarter follows the same approach as the second and third quarters: an initial week of reflection followed by twelve weeks spread over the four Corporate Disciplines, at a suggested pace of three weeks per Discipline. The planning chart offers you the chance to change this arrangement in response to how you feel God is leading you.

The sections with ideas for practicing the respective Corporate Disciplines also follow the standard pattern: questions for further reading and reflection, specific suggestions for practice, Scripture passages and literary quotations to contemplate, and "reflection points" for journal entries.

After the fourth quarter takes you through the end of a full year with the Spiritual Disciplines, this workbook concludes with a "Closing Retreat" (see pages 163–66. The Retreat will guide you through reflecting on your journey as a whole and looking ahead at how the experiences can take hold in your life in a lasting way.

LOOKING BACK

As you are ready to look back at the third quarter, work through the following questions to help you evaluate your experiences. Feel free to skip any questions for which you lack time or interest.

- How would you describe the high points or deepest satisfactions of your experiences in preceding weeks?

- How would you describe the chief struggles or frustrations of your experiences in preceding weeks?

- Which Outward Disciplines were the most enjoyable, and which were the least enjoyable?

- What were the most important insights you learned about yourself and your relationships?

- What were the most important insights you learned about God?

■   Check the response that best describes how you are feeling at this point about your journey through the Spiritual Disciplines:

- ☐   Very positive; eager to move ahead into the final quarter
- ☐   Generally encouraged, with some concerns about integrating practice of the Disciplines in the months ahead
- ☐   Cautious about continuing because of the number of Disciplines that have accumulated by now, which seems burdensome
- ☐   Overwhelmed and in need of a break
- ☐   Tired out from doing this for most of a year
- ☐   Reluctant or hesitant about involvement with others in the practice of the Corporate Disciplines
- ☐   Not sure

Does your response suggest any particular steps you ought to be taking in order to renew your perspective on the journey? (For example: overhaul your expectations and change them accordingly; work through feelings of being overwhelmed by the cumulative number of Disciplines; stop for a few weeks to take a break or to stay on a simple maintenance level before doing something new.) To help you answer this question, talk over your responses with a spiritual companion or group of friends. Draw on the strength and wisdom that God will give you through others.

Everyone needs to take a break from time to time. Richard Foster tells of how, after many months of intensive studying, writing, and practicing the Discipline of prayer, he experienced a time when he could not pray.

"Could not" pray is not exactly correct; "did not want to" is more to the point. I had no heart for prayer. I struggled on for a couple of weeks, trying to make myself do what I had no desire or motivation to do. Then finally I shared with my Spiritual Formation Group what was going on inside me. They extended grace and mercy to me. Their only recommendation was that I end work a little earlier each day and give that time to physical exercise.

That evening as I was jogging, I decided that it would be good for me to rest from any attempts at prayer for one week. Instead I would simply walk/jog an hour each day. I asked my Spiritual Formation Group to pray in my stead. And almost immediately I felt release, knowing that my friends had become my prayer.

The next morning I woke up wanting to pray! Glad for the renewed desire, I did, however, stick to my plan and went throughout my days sustained by the prayers of others. . . . By the next week I was ready to pray again.

LOOKING AHEAD

Based on your evaluations, work through the following questions to help you consider how to focus your journey through the Corporate Disciplines in the next twelve weeks. Answer those questions that seem most helpful to you in gathering your thoughts.

■ What desires and concerns regarding your spiritual growth do you want to address in the weeks ahead?

■ Which Corporate Disciplines are you most eager to explore in greater depth in the months ahead?

■ Which positive experiences from the past twelve weeks do you want to build on?

■ In exploring the Corporate Disciplines, what do you want to do differently from your experiences in exploring the Inward and Outward Disciplines?

■ Look back at your notes and journal entries from Weeks 10 through 13. Are there any specific practices of the Corporate Disciplines you experimented with during those weeks that you want to incorporate in the fourth quarter?

■ Take time to review your "Record of Commitments" in order to identify which goals you want to carry forward into the fourth quarter. Again, treat this step carefully: it is an important pivot point between major segments of your journey. Pray for wisdom and discernment, and seek guidance from others in confirming the directions you choose.

Repeat the following steps:

1. Cross off any commitments you previously recorded that no longer seem important, valuable, or realistic.
2. Comb back through your notes and journal reflections from your exploration of the Outward Disciplines. Look for any desires or goals for ongoing practice of simplicity, solitude, submission, and service that you do want to enter in your "Record of Commitments."
3. Update your "Record of Commitments" accordingly.

PLANNING FOR THE FOURTH QUARTER

The suggested structure shown in the planning chart below allows three weeks of focus for each Corporate Discipline. As you consider whether to plan an alternative structure, take your reflections to a spiritual friend or group of spiritual companions who can help you discern God's leading. If you are exploring these Disciplines in a group context, then make the decision a matter of group discussion and prayer.

After careful consideration, identify your time allotments for the Corporate Disciplines in the next twelve weeks. Note any changes in the right-hand column of the chart below. (Consider pencilling in these notations so you can adjust them in response to the leading of the Holy Spirit in coming weeks.)

Suggested structure	Week	Alternative structure
Confession	41	
	42	
	43	
Worship	44	
	45	
	46	
Guidance	47	
	48	
	49	
Celebration	50	
	51	
	52	

HEADING INTO EACH DISCIPLINE

As you head into the Corporate Disciplines, take time to get an overall perspective on how you want to focus your practice. As you begin each section, follow these four steps to maximize the benefit of the ideas for in-depth exploration of each Corporate Discipline:

1. Read through the ideas listed and familiarize yourself with them. Circle or check those you think you want to use.
2. Refer back to your planning chart above to refresh your memory regarding how many weeks you want to spend with this Discipline.
3. Set goals for what you want to do each week, based on the ideas you circled or checked. If you would rather not keep these goals "in your head," write them down in your journal—perhaps assigning weekly pages for the duration of your focus on this Discipline, with the goals as the heading.

   This exercise will establish a helpful target, even if you shift your specific focus during a given week.
4. Review your "Record of Commitments" for your intentions regarding ongoing practice of other Disciplines. If you desire to integrate any goals listed there with your exploration of meditation in coming weeks, make a note of those goals to the appropriate pages in your journal.

Once you have taken these four steps, you will be well prepared to head into each Corporate Discipline with at least an initial direction for how you want to proceed.

IDEAS FOR WEEKLY PLANNING

At the start of each week, perhaps on Sunday evenings, spend a half-hour getting perspective on where you are in your journey. Your journal will be an invaluable support for this time by giving you a place to write down your reflections and plans. You might simply mark a new page with "Weekly Planning" and the date, so later on you can go back and find it easily.

Here are a few ideas for how to make good use of this weekly review:

1. Take a mini-break by mentally stepping back from your progress through the Spiritual Disciplines. Pause to thank God for grace for the journey.
2. Reflect on the significance of your experiences in the preceding week (the "reflection points" listed at the end of each in-depth Discipline section are intended for this purpose).
3. Check back to your overall plan for the fourth quarter, as you sketched it out in the planning chart above. If you want to shift the time frames you decided on earlier, change the chart accordingly. Also, check your "Record of Commitments" for practice of other Disciplines you want to carry into the week, writing it down if you find it helpful to do so.
4. Review your responses to the questions you answered in the "Looking Ahead" section. Make note of any desires or commitments you want to carry forward into the coming week. If you have assigned weekly pages and written down goals for practicing the current Discipline, review those goals and adjust them if necessary.
5. Throughout the week, keying off your weekly goals, work through the material you have circled or checked in each section. Proceed at whatever pace is comfortable for you. Space has been provided in the individual in-depth Discipline sections for responses and notes, but you may find it helpful to record key insights or experiences in your journal as they occur during the week.

WRAPPING UP HINGE WEEK 40

In your journal or in the space provided below, note any additional thoughts and reflections from this planning week.

Celebrating Confession

God has given us our brothers and sisters to
stand in Christ's stead and make God's
presence and forgiveness real to us.

Celebration of Discipline, p. 147

SUGGESTIONS FOR FURTHER READING OF
CELEBRATION OF DISCIPLINE, Chapter 10

■   Consider the statement, "It is through the voice of our brothers and sisters that the word of forgiveness is heard and takes root in our lives." Based on your personal experiences, can you agree with this statement?

If your answer is "yes," write down any significant events in which you were on the giving and/or the receiving end of this relationship.

If your answer is "no," reflect on why you have not experienced this corporate grace. Do you want to? What changes do you think would be necessary in order for you to give or receive this "word of forgiveness" in the community of spiritual family?

■ Chapter 10 of *Celebration of Discipline* lists three elements as essential to confessing: examination of conscience in identifying concrete sins; sorrow or regret for offending "the heart of the Father"; and a determination to avoid sin, or a yearning for holy living. Would you change this list at all? If so, how?

■ Under what conditions, if any, do you feel God could use you to receive another person's confession?

■ Do you agree that all believers are given authority to proclaim Christ's forgiveness to others? Why or why not?

■ Check your level of comfort or discomfort with the following forms of practicing confession.

	Very Comfortable	Somewhat Comfortable	Not sure	Somewhat Uncomfortable	Very Uncomfortable
The institutionalized Confession, or sacrament of penance	☐	☐	☐	☐	☐
A priest, pastor, minister, or ordained person with authority formally granted by an ecclesiastical institution	☐	☐	☐	☐	☐
A spiritual director, mentor, or adviser	☐	☐	☐	☐	☐
A support group of some kind	☐	☐	☐	☐	☐
Another believer with whom you feel comfortable	☐	☐	☐	☐	☐
A close friend	☐	☐	☐	☐	☐
In private, individually before God	☐	☐	☐	☐	☐

Are you satisfied with all the responses you checked? Or do any of those responses suggest areas in which you would like to change your practice of confession?

SPECIFIC SUGGESTIONS FOR PRACTICING THE DISCIPLINE OF CONFESSION

Consider the following suggestions after reviewing your responses to the questions and ideas in Week 10. As you explore the Corporate Disciplines in depth, ask God to make you aware of any needs you may have for strengthening your participation in the community of faith. (If you tend to be a "loner" in your spiritual life, use this final quarter of your journey through the Disciplines to consider changing patterns of isolation you may have settled into, intentionally or unintentionally.)

■   Reflect on God's forgiveness as our invitation to confession. Specific ways to do this might include the following:

- Meditate on the death of Christ as God's loving sacrifice of forgiveness.
- Study a few key Scripture passages (see list that follows) and memorize two or more of them. Dwell on these passages meditatively and prayerfully.
- Study a classic Christian writer on the subject of sin and forgiveness. Pray for inward illumination as you read.
- Meditate on areas in which you find it difficult to accept God's forgiveness. Set aside times of solitude for listening prayer. Seek guidance from others to help you identify the blockages. Open yourself to experiencing the reality of God's presence and forgiveness through a fellow believer.

■   Enter into a mutual commitment with another believer for regular sessions together in which you will focus on confession, forgiveness, thanksgiving, and praise. As an alternative to discussing issues that come up day-to-day, you might choose to focus your time together on nagging or long-term struggles to find release from self-condemnation or to let go of long-standing bitterness. Together, seek the manifestation of God's transforming work in the joy arising from celebrating the forgiveness of sins.

■   Through your practice of corporate confession, seek the transforming work of the Spirit in preparing you to minister to those who confess sin to you. Seek the help of a spiritual mentor or support group in the following areas:

- Deepening your understanding of the common frailty of the human condition and the boundless grace and mercy of God's acceptance.
- Increasing your ability to keep a confidence.
- Freeing yourself from any impulses to control or "straighten out" others.
- Reflecting the love and grace of God.
- Cultivating the gift of spiritual discernment.
- Practicing listening silence with others.
- Praying for healing in the proclamation of forgiveness and the laying on of hands.

■ Choose a situation in which you carry guilt because of some real or perceived hurt you feel you have caused someone else. Seek the grace and peace of God's forgiveness.

- During a period of solitary prayer, fasting, or meditation, write out as clearly and concisely as possible exactly what the burden is.
- Take this articulation of your burden to a trusted person or persons who can help you deal with it and release it.
- If possible or appropriate, go to the person you feel you have wronged. Confess whatever harm you feel you have done and ask for that person's forgiveness.

SCRIPTURE PASSAGES RELEVANT TO THE PRACTICE OF CONFESSION

Reflect on the following passages prayerfully and in consultation with others to learn how they should guide and inform your practice of the Discipline of confession.

■ Nehemiah 1:4–11 and Daniel 9:4–19 record prayers in which individuals confess not just personal sins but the sins of an entire community and race.

■ Psalm 32:1–5 illuminates the crucial connection between confession and the experience of God's forgiveness.

■ John 20:19–23 records Jesus' post-resurrection appearance to his disciples, in which he commissioned them for ministry and granted them authority to forgive sins in his name or to withhold this ministry of forgiveness.

■ James 5:16 calls us to confession in community.

■ 1 John 1:5–10 teaches central truths about the universality of sin, the importance of confession, and the assurance of forgiveness.

THOUGHTS FOR CONTEMPLATION

Reflect on the following quotations to stimulate and inform your practice of confession.

> So far as I am concerned, what has most often opened my eyes to my own unconscious sin is the witness of friends when they have told me about their own faults. This, let it be noticed is the complete opposite of judgment. Instead of denouncing my guilt, they spoke to me of their own, and an amazing light flashed into the depths of my heart. An inward voice murmured, "This is true of myself, but I have never recognized it."

Sometimes people speak to us about their faults in order to teach us and to provoke deliberately this movement of self-awareness. But then we feel that behind their apparent humility they are judging us, and that in fact they are boasting of being better able to recognize their errors than we ourselves are, and we react in the contrary direction by justifying ourselves.

But if their testimony is truly humble, spontaneous, living, without ulterior motives, if it is a genuine word of acknowledgment by those who have found the true solution, who have discovered the grace of God, then it draws us also in turn into the same experience, which is the greatest experience a man can undergo.

PAUL TOURNIER

If you wish to climb to this height, you must begin bravely and lay the axe to the root; pull up and destroy every movement toward self-centered, selfish desires. All that must be radically overcome is rooted in this vice of making yourself the center of your own world. When this evil is mastered and brought under control, great peace and calm will follow. But because few people strive to rise above themselves in such a way, they remain entangled in a fibery web and their spirits can never soar on high.

THOMAS À KEMPIS

So the strange fatality in our human life and the life of nations is that it is always basing itself on the other person's guilt and forgetting to beat its own breast. And our world will never find peace, neither nations nor individuals in their private and vocational lives will ever find peace as long as only the cry for vengeance is heard among us and as long as we are not ready for reconciliation: Forgive us our debts!

HELMUT THIELICKE

For the present moment it is the "I" alone that matters. It is the "I" that sets the stage for our act of contrition. It indicates that I am taking responsibility for what follows: that *I* am confessing it. It is not "we"; I do not share with others what I am going to confess. I speak it *to* them, as we will see, but I speak only *for* myself.

JEFFREY SOBOSAN

REFLECTION POINTS FOR JOURNAL ENTRIES

Use the following "reflection points" as you find them helpful for exploring your experiences with the Discipline of confession.

- *Reflection point:* How is the practice of confession leading you into a deeper experience of intimacy with God?

- *Reflection point:* In what ways, if any, has confession enabled you to experience joy and freedom in community?

- *Reflection point:* What disappointments or disillusionments, if any, have you experienced in practicing confession in community?

- *Reflection point:* What has your practice of confession been teaching you about yourself and your relationships?

- *Reflection point:* What insights or struggles about the character of God has your practice of confession brought to light?

- *Reflection point:* In what ways, if any, has your practice of confession been guided or supported by other Spiritual Disciplines?

- *Reflection point:* In what areas do you especially desire God's guidance and grace for practicing confession as a Corporate Discipline?

Celebrating Worship

Worship is our response to the overtures of
love from the heart of the Father.

Celebration of Discipline, p. 158

SUGGESTIONS FOR FURTHER READING OF
CELEBRATION OF DISCIPLINE, Chapter 11

■   What is it that most often prompts in you a desire to worship God?

■   What are the primary effects in your life of your practice of worship?

■ Think back to any experiences you have had of "what the biblical writers called *koinonia*, deep inward fellowship in the power of the Spirit." Do you participate in this *koinonia* regularly? If not, what is hindering you from doing so?

■ What kinds of obstacles most often prevent you from participating in worship the way you want to?

■ Foster lists three divinely appointed avenues into worship: (1) a perpetual, inward, listening silence; (2) the movement of our spirit in praise, often focused through music; (3) bodily participation, in a variety of physical postures consistent with our inner spirit, as a part of wholehearted worship. Are these avenues part of your worship of God? Why or why not?

SPECIFIC SUGGESTIONS FOR PRACTICING THE DISCIPLINE OF WORSHIP

Review your notes from Week 11 as you consider the following suggestions for worship. If you are not part of a body of believers who meet together regularly, perhaps now would be a good time to pursue involvement in a local congregation or fellowship. Worship is a gift of God intended for God's people to participate in corporately in the unity of the Spirit. As we suspend the clamor and preoccupation of our individual lives to draw together in expectant adoration, worship becomes a primary channel for experiencing the reality of this divine unity.

Sometimes it helps to remember that we gather for worship as participants seeking to enter into active communion with God and each other, not spectators coming to be gratified or entertained. Although worship can make us feel good, that is properly a byproduct, not a goal. The true goal of worship is to respond with our whole selves to God's self-revelation in love. This recognition of who God is and what God has done for us is the origin of our joy and freedom in worship.

■ If you are not currently participating regularly in worship with other believers, consider the following steps:

- Set aside at least one or two sessions for reflection and prayer. Study key Scripture passages about worship (consult the list that follows and the many references cited in Chapter 11 of *Celebration of Discipline*). Additionally, consult classic Christian writers on this subject. Ask God to give you insight into why you have chosen not to worship with other believers and when you should take steps to change this situation.
- Take your reflections to a close friend or spiritual adviser. Ask that person to respond to where you are now and how you ought to be thinking about growth in worship.
- Choose two or three different churches or congregations of believers and visit one each week. Before going, prepare by praying for an experience of the Spirit touching your spirit, for genuine encounter with other people in the service, and for guidance regarding whether you should become a regular participant. Talk to a friend or adviser afterward to help get perspective on your responses.
- Gather a small group of people together for an informal session of worship and praise.

■ Focus on preparation for worship by choosing one or more of the following ideas:

- Practice intercessory prayer for the human worship leaders in your next gathering. Ask Christ to draw you and others into intimate communion with God as the gifts of the Spirit are exercised and received.
- If possible, obtain Scripture texts for the service in advance. Read and study them before you gather for worship. Dwell on them prayerfully in the days leading up to your gathering.
- Cultivate a holy expectancy by developing a worshipful spirit in the week prior to your gathering. (See the specific suggestions in Chapter 11 of *Celebration of Discipline*—first edition, pp. 141–43; revised edition, pp. 162–64.)
- Fast for a period of time before the worship service in order to center on contemplative adoration of God. Plan to break your fast after worship with a few others (who may also choose to fast in preparation with you). Celebrate God's good gifts—chief among them your common life in Christ. (This practice is well-suited as preparation for receiving the Eucharist or attending a service of Holy Communion.)

- Get together for worship with another person. Begin with confession as a way of cleansing your spirits. (Consider how the other Disciplines—such as meditation, prayer, fasting, and solitude—can be combined with this confession.) Then enter worship with thanksgiving for God's gracious forgiveness in Christ.

■ Seek a more intense and vital participation in worship in one or more of the following ways:

- Practice a perpetual, inward, listening silence in the opening minutes of the service. If your worship gathering does not include time set aside for quiet preparation, arrive early and spend ten minutes in silent, meditative prayer.
- Select a Scripture passage that stimulates the movement of your spirit in thanksgiving and adoration. Memorize it prior to worship. As you enter into the worship gathering, dwell on this truth as an avenue for entering into the Presence of God in praise.
- During worship, ask God to free you to worship with your whole being—body, mind, spirit, and emotions. Be receptive to the guidance of the Spirit in the form of your worship—physical posture, singing, speaking or remaining silent, and so on.
- Practice prayer without ceasing during the duration of your worship gathering. As you notice particular individuals, engage in "flash prayers" that God would renew and refresh them. Ask that worship leaders would receive guidance, discernment, and a deepened awareness of the Presence of God. Pray that everyone gathered together would experience the movement of the Holy Spirit during worship. Ask God to bless the effects of worship in sending each person back into his or her daily routines in the coming week with a more vital witness to the love of God.
- Participate in the tradition of treating Sunday as the Sabbath (originally established by divine appointment as the seventh day of the Jewish week) by setting apart the whole day for worship, rest, and recreation.

■ Choose one or more ideas from the seven "Steps into Worship" listed in Chapter 11 of *Celebration of Discipline*. Spend several weeks practicing that idea as a way of growing in your participation in worship. If you experimented positively with one of these steps in Week 11, you may want to continue with it now in greater depth—or try one or two others.

■ Reflect on the fruits of worship by focusing on the following statement in your practice of the Spiritual Disciplines over the next few weeks: "To worship is to change." Pray for the transforming work of the Spirit in giving you a deeper desire for holy obedience. Seek God's guidance and the guidance of others in discerning how and where to pursue this change.

SCRIPTURE PASSAGES RELEVANT TO THE PRACTICE OF WORSHIP

Scripture is filled with references to the praise and adoration that God's people are to enjoy. Reflect on the following passages prayerfully and in consultation with others to understand and apply their insights into how we are to worship God. (See also the references cited in Chapter 11 of *Celebration of Discipline*.)

- Exodus 20:1–17 records the giving of God's Law to Israel: the Decalogue, or the Ten Commandments. See especially verses 2–6 for the primacy of worship.

- Deuteronomy 4:32–39, part of Moses' great parting speech to the Israelites, calls God's people to reflect on who God is and the miraculous nature of God's deeds.

- 1 Chronicles 16:8–36 and Psalm 100 are two of many recorded psalms of worship and praise.

- In John 4:24, Jesus describes the kind of worship that God desires us to offer.

- Colossians 3:11–17 provides instructions for the common life to which we are called, including the kinds of worship we are encouraged to offer to God in the gathered fellowship.

- Revelation prophetically pictures the ultimate and eternal worship for which we were created. See especially: 4:1–5:14, 19:6–9, and 21:1–4.

THOUGHTS FOR CONTEMPLATION

Reflect on the following quotations to stimulate and inform your practice of worship.

> The allegorical sense of her great action dawned on me the other day. The precious alabaster box which one must *break* over the Holy Feet is one's *heart*. Easier said than done. And the contents become perfume only when it is broken. While they are safe inside they are more like sewage. All very alarming.
>
> C. S. LEWIS

> . . . when I came into the silent assemblies of God's people, I felt a secret power among them, which touched my heart. And as I gave way to it, I found the evil in me weakening, and the good lifted up. Thus it was that I was knit into them and united with them. And I hungered more and more for the increase of this power and life until I could feel myself perfectly redeemed.
>
> ROBERT BARCLAY

With diligence meet together and with diligence wait to feel the Lord God to arise, to scatter and expel all that which is the cause of leanness and barrenness upon any soul; for it is the Lord [who] must do it, and he will be waited upon in sincerity and fervency of spirit.

STEPHEN CRISP

O my God, O love, love thyself in me! . . . Thy love is tyrannical. It never says, "It is enough." The more it is given, the more it asks. It even treats the faithful soul with a sort of treason. First it draws it by its gentleness. Then it becomes stern toward it. And at last it hides itself to give it a mortal blow, by taking away all visible support. O incomprehensible God, I adore thee! Thou hast made me for thyself alone.

FRANÇOIS FÉNELON

REFLECTION POINTS FOR JOURNAL ENTRIES

Use the following "reflection points" as you find them helpful for exploring your experiences with the Discipline of worship.

- *Reflection point:* How is the practice of worship leading you into a deeper experience of intimacy with God?
- *Reflection point:* In what ways, if any, have you experienced joy and freedom in worship through practicing it in community?
- *Reflection point:* What disappointments or frustrations, if any, have you experienced in participating in corporate worship?
- *Reflection point:* What has your practice of worship been teaching you about yourself and your relationships?
- *Reflection point:* What has your practice of worship been teaching you about life in community with other believers?
- *Reflection point:* What has your practice of worship been teaching you about God?
- *Reflection point:* In what ways, if any, has your practice of worship been guided or strengthened by other Spiritual Disciplines?
- *Reflection point:* In what areas do you especially desire God's guidance and grace for growing in the Discipline of worship?

Celebrating Guidance

[Paul] saw that the gifts of the Spirit were
given by the Spirit to the body in such a way
that interdependence was ensured. No one
person possessed everything. Even the most
mature needed the help of others. The most
insignificant had something to contribute. No
one could hear the whole counsel of God in
isolation.

Celebration of Discipline, p. 179

SUGGESTIONS FOR FURTHER READING OF
CELEBRATION OF DISCIPLINE, Chapter 12

■   Have you ever been part of a group in which you and others received divine
guidance through the group experience? If so, how did you confirm that the
leading was from God, rather than from the collective outcome of human opinion?

■ Chapter 12 presents several stories and models of God's guidance through groups. Can you identify with any elements in these stories, based on your personal experience?

  • Israel at the time of the Exodus—a people under the common rule of God, with a divinely appointed leader.
  • The apostles and the early church in Acts—a gathered community united by a common commitment and mission, under the direct rule of the Spirit, using Disciplines such as prayer, fasting, and worship as they sought the Lord's instruction together.
  • St. Francis of Assisi—discerning the mind of Christ through spiritual counsel from at least two trusted friends.
  • The Church of the Saviour—identifying God's call to service in the context of group worship, prayer, and free interaction.
  • Seeking confirmation for critical decisions, such as marriage, through the response of the believing community.
  • The Society of Friends in colonial America—receiving guidance for a business or organization through structured corporate meetings.

■ What aspects of your spiritual growth right now do you think could benefit most from a relationship with a spiritual director?

■ In what contexts, if any, have you provided spiritual direction or guidance to others? What were some of the most significant insights or lessons you learned from these experiences?

■ In your opinion, what are the best safeguards or checkpoints for identifying when someone has reached a limit of corporate guidance?

SPECIFIC SUGGESTIONS FOR PRACTICING THE DISCIPLINE OF GUIDANCE

Guidance is a gift we receive rather than a task we accomplish. Therefore, our proper posture in this Discipline is one of open hands in a mode of receptivity—recognizing that we are not in control, waiting to be surprised by God through the grace of community.

As you consider the following ideas for practice, review your experiences from Week 12.

■ If you feel in need of identifying a spiritual director or mentor who will enter into a relationship of mutual growth with you, begin praying this week that God will identify this person to you—and that whoever is to become this person will also experience the stirring of the Spirit. Consider these steps of preparation:

- Review the characteristics listed in *Celebration of Discipline* regarding this relationship (see Chapter 12, "The Spiritual Director").
- Ask God to give you wisdom and sensitivity regarding your own needs and motives.

  It could be that you have already taken steps to begin such a relationship. If so, pray for sensitivity to the Spirit as you pursue how to develop the relationship as a conduit of God's guidance.

■ Read a good book on spiritual guidance, and spend several weeks studying it. Make your reading an active participation by taking notes, thinking critically and posing questions, looking up Scripture references, and so on. Ask those with whom you are in a guidance relationship to read the book as well. Get together a few times to discuss your insights and questions. (Possible books mentioned in *Celebration of Discipline* include: Tilden H. Edwards, *Spiritual Friend: Reclaiming the Gift of Spiritual Direction*; Henri Nouwen, *The Way of the Heart*; and Barry A. Woodbridge, *A Guidebook for Spiritual Friends*.)

■ In any current relationship you may have with an individual or group, discuss how to encourage each other in deepening your sensitivity to the corporate leading of the Spirit. As a way to initiate or focus your dialogue, you might select an issue, question, Scripture reference, or excerpt from your reading in *Celebration of Discipline.* Consider also a study in the Book of Acts.

■ If you are part of a group or in a relational commitment right now in which the Discipline of corporate guidance is practiced, ask God to reveal to you this week one step you might take to strengthen your contribution to the life of this community. For example:

  • Identify personal issues you need to work through in order to deepen the genuineness of your interaction with others.
  • Seek God's leading in exercising a spiritual gift you have been withholding.
  • Ask for the group's response to a particular issue or decision you are facing.
  • Take action on a decision regarding some level of group involvement that you have been contemplating recently.
  • In sensitivity to the guidance of the Spirit, address an unresolved issue that you may have left hanging with someone in the group. (The Inward Disciplines may be helpful here in preparation for conducting a meeting or opening a dialogue.)

■ If God is using you in some way to provide spiritual direction for others, whether regularly or sporadically, set aside several sessions for meditation, prayer, and guidance to evaluate how you are remaining open to be used by God in this kind of ministry. Search out the answers to such questions as:

  • "Do I stay up to date on the social needs and forces that are shaping or pressuring the lives of individuals around me?"
  • "Am I increasingly sensitive to where others are in their spiritual journey?"
  • "Do I stay honest with myself about where I am spiritually and emotionally, and am I willing to be honest and vulnerable with others?"
  • "Do I pray carefully, compassionately, and earnestly about those who look to me for guidance?"
  • "Am I aware that guidance is a two-way relationship, with Jesus as our ever-present Teacher?"
  • "Do I have resources in others who can advise me about giving spiritual direction?"
  • "Do I rely on the leading of the Holy Spirit, the Scriptures, and the testimony of the body of Christ to inform how I advise others, rather than on my own easily arrived at opinions?"

SCRIPTURE PASSAGES RELEVANT TO THE PRACTICE OF GUIDANCE

Much of the Bible recounts stories of divine revelation and leading through and within the community of God's people. The following Scriptures are just a few of the many passages rich in insights for the corporate practice of guidance.

■ Proverbs 27:17 graphically pictures the growth that takes place in community.

■ Matthew 18:19–20 proclaims the assurance of divine presence and the power of divine guidance for believers gathered in Jesus' name.

■ Acts 2:1–4 recounts the commissioning of gathered believers on Pentecost. The entire book of Acts provides numerous models of divine guidance in the community of faith. For example:

  • Conviction of sin—Ananias and Sapphira, 5:1–11.
  • Faithfulness during persecution—the apostles before the Sanhedrin, 5:17–42.
  • Distribution of tasks in community ministry—the choosing of the seven, 6:1–7.
  • Direction and focus of ministry—Peter and Cornelius, 10:1–48.
  • Sending out members on mission—Paul and Barnabus, 13:1–3.
  • Resolving divisive issues—the council at Jerusalem, 15:1–35.

■ 1 Corinthians 10:23–11:1 provides guidelines for Christian freedom based on what will benefit others both inside and outside the community of faith.

■ Galatians 6:1–10 teaches individual responsibility within the context of the shared life of Christian community.

THOUGHTS FOR CONTEMPLATION

Reflect on the following quotations to stimulate and inform your practice of guidance.

> Divine guidance cannot be ours as a reliable and intelligible fact of life except when seen as one aspect of God's presence with us and of His life in us. Only our *communion* with God provides the appropriate context of *communications* between us and Him. And within those communications *guidance* is given in a manner suitable to our particular lives and circumstances and to our life together with Him in His earthly and heavenly family.
>
> DALLAS WILLARD

And when all my hopes in them and in all men were gone, so that I had nothing outwardly to help me, nor could tell what to do, then, oh then, I heard a voice which said, "There is one, even Christ Jesus, that can speak to thy condition," and when I heard it my heart did leap for joy. Then the Lord did let me see why there was none upon the earth that could speak to my condition, namely, that I might give him all the glory . . . that Jesus Christ might have the pre-eminence, who enlightens, and gives grace, and faith, and power.

GEORGE FOX

O Thou who alone knowest what lies before me this day, grant that in every hour of it I may stay close to Thee. Let me be in the world, yet not of it. Let me use this world without abusing it. If I buy, let me be as though I possessed not. If I have nothing, let me be as though possessing all things. Let me today embark on no undertaking that is not in line with Thy will for my life, nor shrink from any sacrifice which Thy will may demand. Suggest, direct, control every movement of my mind; for my Lord Christ's sake. Amen.

JOHN BAILLIE

Lord you are great, and most worthy of praise; great is your worth and your wisdom beyond reckoning. And man, a fragment of your creation, desires to praise you—man, carrying round with him his own mortality, carrying round with him the witness of his sin and the witness that you "resist the proud," yet desires to praise you, he, a fragment of your creation. You prompt him to take delight in praising you, because you made us for yourself, and our heart is restless until it find rest in you. Grant to me, Lord, to know and understand whether I should first call upon you or praise you, and to know you before I call on you. But who calls on you without knowing you? Not knowing you, he could call upon something other than you are. Or is it rather that you are called upon in order to be known? But "how shall they call upon one in whom they have not believed? or how shall they believe without one to preach?" And they shall praise the Lord who seek, for if they seek him they find him, and finding him shall praise him. I shall seek you, Lord, by calling upon you, and may I call upon you because I believed on you, for you have been made known to us. My faith calls upon you, Lord, the faith you gave to me, which you breathed into me, through the humanity of your son and the ministry of your preacher.

SAINT AUGUSTINE

REFLECTION POINTS FOR JOURNAL ENTRIES

Use the following "reflection points" as you find them helpful for exploring your experiences with the Discipline of guidance.

- *Reflection point:* How is the practice of guidance leading you into a deeper experience of intimacy with God?

- *Reflection point:* In what ways, if any, have you experienced joy and freedom in the corporate practice of guidance?

- *Reflection point:* What disappointments or hurts, if any, have you experienced in giving or receiving guidance as a Corporate Discipline?

- *Reflection point:* What has your practice of guidance been teaching you about yourself and your relationships?

- *Reflection point:* What has your practice of guidance been teaching you about life in community with other believers?

- *Reflection point:* What has your practice of guidance been teaching you about God?

- *Reflection point:* In what ways, if any, has your practice of guidance been strengthened or informed by other Spiritual Disciplines?

- *Reflection point:* In what areas do you especially desire God's leading and grace for growing in the Discipline of guidance?

Celebrating Celebration

The decision to set the mind on the higher
things of life is an act of the will. That is
why celebration is a Discipline. It is not
something that falls on our heads. It is the
result of a consciously chosen way of
thinking and living. When we choose this
way, the healing and redemption in Christ
will break into the inner recesses of our lives
and relationships, and the inevitable
result will be joy.

Celebration of Discipline, p. 195

SUGGESTIONS FOR FURTHER READING OF
CELEBRATION OF DISCIPLINE, Chapter 13

- "Freedom from anxiety and care forms the basis for celebration. Because we know [God] cares for us, we can cast all our care upon him. God has turned our mourning into dancing." How do you think this statement might provide insight into the difference between (1) *eliminating* anxiety, care, and mourning, and (2) *transforming* or *redeeming* anxiety, care, and mourning?

■ In what areas of your life is it hardest for you to choose to place carefree trust in God's ability to meet all your needs?

■ How might celebration of the wonder and glory of God, especially as manifested in our enjoyment of "the good things of the earth," help keep us from taking ourselves—and even our problems—too seriously?

■ In what ways can celebration as a corporate Discipline strengthen us during times when the difficulties of life leach the joy from our spirit?

■ In your opinion, how is celebration properly at the center of all the Spiritual Disciplines?

SPECIFIC SUGGESTIONS FOR PRACTICING THE DISCIPLINE OF CELEBRATION

Your practice of celebration at this point in your journey can involve looking back as well as looking ahead. You can look back in joyful recognition of the transforming work of God to which you have opened up your life through the Spiritual Disciplines. You can look ahead in trust that God is at work in your journey of growth to draw you ever more deeply into the abundant freedom of life in the Spirit. In this context, celebrations of the present moment can be truly joyful and carefree.

As you consider the following suggestions for practice, review any celebratory steps you took in Week 13. Remember that a refreshed perspective and a keen awareness of the goodness of life comes to us most freely in community.

■ Choose a quiet place for a time of solitary reflection on the following question: "In what ways am I aware of God's transforming work in my life during my journey through the Disciplines?" As you reflect on your experiences, review your journal entries during the time you have spent with this workbook. Look for attitudinal and behavioral changes. Notice how your responses to people and circumstances may have shifted.

Write your thoughts down, perhaps in your journal reflections. Then share them with someone—a close friend, a spiritual mentor, a group—who can help you affirm and celebrate the work of God in your life.

■ Set aside one or two sessions of solitude to identify the area(s) of your life in which you cannot celebrate. Consider writing them out in the form of prayers or psalms. As you are able and willing to share these difficult places with another person or persons, draw upon their strength of companionship and spiritual affirmation to help you look ahead for the light of God's grace as you walk through the shadows. Perhaps there are ways they can celebrate *for* you until you come to a place where they can celebrate *with* you.

A helpful image here comes from Psalm 84:5–7, which describes God's people in pilgrimage together:

Happy are those whose strength is in you,
    in whose heart are the highways to Zion.
As they pass through the valley of Baca,
    they make it a place of springs;
    the early rain also covers it with pools.
They go from strength to strength;
    the God of gods will be seen in Zion.

■ Get together with several others for a few celebration gatherings. Look for ways to participate in "singing, dancing, or noise-making"—or any other form of celebration—in a spirit of thanksgiving and praise. You might choose to focus your time on something specific to your experiences, or, alternatively, on the ways in which you see manifestations of a general scriptural theme, such as:

• God's ability to provide for all our needs (Ps. 66; Eph. 3:20–21; Phil. 4:19).
• God's good gifts (Matt. 7:7–11; Phil. 4:8; James 1:17).

- Have a dinner party to celebrate the pleasurable discoveries of people getting to know each other—whether as individuals meeting each other for the first time, or acquaintances and friends getting to know each other better. Consider the following ideas:
  - a loosely structured gathering for spontaneous conversation
  - a planned structure of individual participation—each person bringing a favorite poem, literary excerpt, or passage to read aloud between dinner and dessert; a multi-course meal with an act of worship led by a different individual between each course; during dinner, individuals take turns sharing personal anecdotes from their lives
  - a meal organized around a seasonal or holiday theme

- Commit yourself to "relax and enjoy the good things of the earth" regularly over the next few weeks, especially as an antidote to chronic seriousness or a tired perspective. Choose one or more areas from the list of suggestions in Chapter 13 of *Celebration of Discipline* (see the section "The Practice of Celebration") in which you can indulge a "carefree spirit of joyous festivity."

  There are many ways to go about this practice of celebration: inject a spirit of celebration into the Disciplines you practice regularly; build in one light-hearted activity each week; spend several weeks preparing for an upcoming holiday or holy day; focus on a creative activity for one or more months; plan creative ways to recognize significant events in the lives of your family or friends.

SCRIPTURE PASSAGES RELEVANT TO THE PRACTICE OF CELEBRATION

Scripture begins in wonder and ends in praise—a celebration of the creative and redeeming work of God wide enough to stretch across all of human history and deep enough to contain all the tragedy, mystery, and glory of individual human lives, centrally that of the God-man, Jesus Christ. Following are just a few of the passages throughout the Bible that call us to the joyful living that is made possible by God's loving faithfulness.

- Exodus 15:1–21 celebrates the Israelites' deliverance from the Egyptian pharaoh's army.
- 2 Samuel 6:1–23 pictures a joyful celebration. Two twists in the story illuminate our calling to obedience and to participation in the rejoicing community.
- Psalm 126 is a moving and lyrical testimony to how the great deeds of the Lord call forth joy from sorrow.

- Luke 4:18–19 records Jesus' announcement that he had come to fulfill Isaiah's prophecy that the Messiah would set humanity free from the bondage of sin and all its consequences.

- John 2:1–11 records the celebration of the wedding feast in which Jesus turned water into wine.

- John 15:11 and 16:20–24, part of Jesus' moving counsel to his disciples in their final hours together before his arrest and death, speak of the joy God wants us to experience.

- Galatians 5:22–23 lists the fruit of the Spirit: the evidence of God's transforming work in our lives.

- Hebrews 12:1–3 calls us to follow Jesus in persevering with a joy that is stronger than even the most grievous suffering and death.

THOUGHTS FOR CONTEMPLATION

Reflect on the following quotations to stimulate and inform your practice of celebration.

God does not die on the day when we cease to believe in a personal deity, but we die on the day when our lives cease to be illumined by the steady radiance, renewed daily, of a wonder, the source of which is beyond all reason.

DAG HAMMARSKJÖLD

Whenever we mount into God's chariots the same thing happens to us spiritually that happened to Elijah. We shall have a translation. Not into the heavens above us, as Elijah did, but into the heaven within us; and this, after all, is almost a grander translation than his. We shall be carried away from the low, early, groveling plane of life, where everything hurts and everything is unhappy, up into the "heavenly places in Christ Jesus," where we can ride in triumph over all below.

HANNAH WHITALL SMITH

There are those who would consider it a strange collection of musical instruments for a monastic liturgy. There is an organ, of course, but . . . the organ is not the only instrument on which we depend for Eucharistic services. On the contrary. There's a set of handbells and a pack of guitars and a grand piano and a harpsichord and a hammered dulcimer and a flute and a trumpet and a recorder and a bass guitar and a harp and a xylophone and dozens of finger bells. I love the music that comes from all those variations, but more than that I love what the grouping itself says about the place of the person in community. . . .

All of them love what they're doing. And all of them are doing it for the sake of the community as well as for their own pleasure. All of them are using their gifts together in praise of God. All of them respect one another's talents, none of them expects to be the whole show, and each of them knows that without the others her own contributions will fail.

JOAN CHITTISTER

Old men rarely sing out loud, but an inner melody warmed (Balthazar's) heart as he shuffled silently toward the caravan. This inner music spilled through every fissure of his bent frame: it came not from the stars, but their Maker. "Wise men know the best songs," thought Balthazar. "The heart can keep a melody even when the stars doubt it."

CALVIN MILLER

REFLECTION POINTS FOR JOURNAL ENTRIES

Use the following "reflection points" as you find them helpful for exploring your experiences with the Discipline of celebration.

- *Reflection point:* How is the practice of celebration leading you into a deeper experience of intimacy with God?

- *Reflection point:* Where has celebration been present in your practice of the Spiritual Disciplines?

- *Reflection point:* Where has celebration been most noticeably absent in your practice of the Spiritual Disciplines?

- *Reflection point:* What has your practice of celebration been teaching you about yourself and your relationships?

- *Reflection point:* What has your practice of celebration been teaching you about life in community with other believers?

- *Reflection point:* What has your practice of celebration been teaching you about God?

- *Reflection point:* In what ways, if any, has your practice of celebration been guided or informed by other Spiritual Disciplines?

- *Reflection point:* In what areas do you especially desire God's leading and grace for growing in "carefree gaiety and a sense of thanksgiving"?

Closing
Retreat

The following outline provides a suggested structure for a two-day retreat. You may choose to depart from these suggestions according to time considerations and personal interest. However you decide to spend time in retreat, you will most likely find it beneficial as a way to reach some sense of closure for this phase of your journey through the Disciplines and develop a fresh anticipation for those phases that now lie ahead.

Purpose: The only reason for a retreat is to be available to God. Everything else is wholly secondary. You are seeking to create an open, empty space in your life where God can work. Therefore, it is imperative to resist the temptation to over-schedule the time. The key is not how much you read or how much you pray, but how available you are.

So stand firm against the powerful urge to pack in lots of activity . . . even religious activity . . . especially religious activity! You are meeting with God, and you will want to enter the cosmic patience of the Eternal. The key in retreat is to "show up and shut up"!

Scripture Meditation: Throughout your retreat you will want to reflect prayerfully on various Scripture passages. As you read these Scriptures, seek to use all your senses. If, for example, you are considering Christ on trial for his life, seek to "see" the crowd, "hear" the accusations, "feel" the sting of the whip. The point of using the sense is to move from "reading about" to "entering in." As you are seeing, hearing, smelling, tasting, touching the story, you will discover that it is your story as well. God will show you, perhaps, that you too are in the crowd jeering "Crucify him!" or, maybe, one of those who speak out accusations against the Holy One.

As you engage in this prayer-filled reading God will lead you to various responses: confession, repentance, awe, worship, adoration, joy. Follow these powerful leadings of the Spirit.

Place: Whenever possible it is best to get away from your normal surroundings of home and work. The reason for this is simply that in your home or at your office, obligations and responsibilities constantly scream for your attention—the laundry needs to be done, letters need to be answered, the door needs to be fixed.

Many retreat centers will accommodate a private retreatant, though usually Catholic facilities are better equipped for this than are Protestant ones. Some Centers have special hermitages or "Poustinias" for personal silent retreat. Camping is also possible though usually less desirable simply because of all the necessary physical arrangements. A motel is the least agreeable arrangement but it can be used if other options are not possible. The key is to be free of the demands of the telephone and the distractions of the media. It helps to have a place where you are able to take long walks if the weather allows. Beyond this it matters little whether you go to the ocean, the mountains, the desert, or the solitude of the urban crowd.

Materials: Notebook or journal, *Celebration of Discipline* book and workbook, study Bible, hymnal or songbook. Other possibilities: musical instruments, art materials, exercise equipment, picnic supplies.

A Note on Procedure: If you are going on this retreat alone, work through the suggestions at your own pace, modifying them according to your needs and desires for this time away. When you return from the retreat, consider sharing your insights and experiences with a friend or spiritual companion.

If you are part of a group retreat, adapt the suggestions as you alternate between time together and time apart. Take turns selecting worship activities. For the study and reflection ideas, consider breaking up into smaller groups of two or three people, alternating the combinations, for discussing your responses.

   I. Opening
      A. Worship—choose any of the following:
         1. Sing one or two hymns of praise and thanksgiving.
         2. Make a list of the top ten things for which you are thankful right now and offer a prayer of gratitude for them.
         3. Read aloud a passage of Scripture that praises God or affirms God's care for us—Psalm 100, 103, or 145; Isaiah 55; Ephesians 1.

B. Reflection on the Journey
  1. In what sense is your journey ending?
  2. In what sense is your journey beginning?

II. Looking Back
  A. Worship—what are the major insights you gained into the character of God? Choose any of the following as a way to respond to them in worship:
    1. Look up one or two key Scripture passages that correspond to these insights and read them aloud.
    2. Choose a corresponding hymn and sing it.
    3. Write out a psalm of praise expressing these insights and read it aloud.
  B. Prayer—respond to these insights, Scriptures, and songs. Spend time in meditative prayer to quiet your mind, heart, and spirit for reflecting back on your journey.
  C. Solitary Study and Meditation—choose any of the following questions or exercises that will help you reflect on the significant experiences of your journey.
    1. In what ways has your journey through the Spiritual Disciplines led you into a deeper experience of intimacy with God?
    2. In what ways, if any, were your expectations of intimacy with God disappointed or left unsatisfied?
    3. What are the most important insights you gained about yourself and your relationships?
    4. Where did you experience the greatest joy?
    5. Where did you experience the greatest frustration or difficulty?
    6. Is there anything you wish you had done differently? Why or why not?
    7. Read back through your journal notes and reflections. Circle or put a star next to the entries that seem most important to you now.
  D. Summary Reflection—describe the major ways in which your journey through the Disciplines affected your life.

III. Looking Ahead
  A. Worship—begin to cultivate a "holy expectancy" for fresh discovery of the character of God. Which aspects of God's character do you especially want to experience or gain a deeper knowledge of in this season of your life? Choose any of the following to express this desire:
    1. Read aloud a Scripture passage that voices this desire.
    2. Sing a hymn that expresses this desire.

      3. Write out a prayer asking God to make himself known to you in this way, and offer it to God.

  B. Prayer—spend time in listening prayer, asking God to direct your thoughts toward those needs and desires regarding your spiritual growth that you should be focusing on for the future.

  C. Solitary Study and Meditation—choose any of the following questions or exercises that will help you reflect on directions you want to move into as a result of your journey.

      1. What desires and concerns regarding your spiritual growth do you want to address in the future?

      2. Which Spiritual Disciplines are you most eager to continue practicing?

      3. Which Spiritual Disciplines are you least eager to continue practicing?

      4. Without worrying about how to integrate them, jot down which practices of the Disciplines you want to maintain in the future. Write down all that come to your mind.

      5. Now make a list of (1) practices you want to continue regularly (daily, weekly, monthly), and (2) practices you want to continue periodically (when you feel the need arises, once every few months, coinciding with special seasons or occasions).

      6. Review your "Record of Commitments." Update it according to the needs and desires that have emerged from your time of study and meditation.

  D. Summary Reflection—describe the major ways in which you want your future journey through the Disciplines to affect your life.

IV. Celebration—choose any of the following:

  A. Leave notebooks behind and go outside for a long walk to enjoy the beauty of God's creation. Let your thoughts settle out until you feel mentally clear and refreshed. Explore the world around you.

  B. Spend time in a spontaneous session of singing or playing instruments.

  C. Celebrate Holy Communion.

  D. Have a picnic or go out to eat somewhere. Put aside thoughts of plans and practices. Relax, laugh, and enjoy each other's company.

  E. Engage in some form of exercise or physical game.

Record of Commitments

Date	Commitments

Date	Commitments

Date	Commitments

Date	Commitments

Date	Commitments

Date	Commitments

Notes

Week 1

Karl Barth, *Dogmatics in Outline,* trans. Walter M. Mosse (New York: Harper & Row, 1959), pp. 138, 140.

Week 2

Donald G. Bloesch, *The Struggle of Prayer* (Colorado Springs: Helmers & Howard, 1988), p. 120.

Week 3

Emilie Griffin, *Clinging: The Experience of Prayer* (San Francisco: Harper & Row, 1984), p. 1.

Week 4

Dallas Willard, *The Spirit of the Disciplines* (San Francisco: Harper & Row, 1988), p. 166.

Week 5

Mortimer J. Adler, *How to Read a Book* (New York: Simon and Schuster, 1972), p. 11.

Week 6

Richard J. Foster, *Freedom of Simplicity* (San Francisco: Harper & Row, 1981), pp. 3–4.

Week 7

Henri J. M. Nouwen, *The Way of the Heart* (New York: Ballantine Books, 1981), pp. 13–14.

Week 8

Charles de Foucauld in *The Lord of the Journey: A Reader in Christian Spirituality,* ed. Roger Pooley and Philip Seddon (San Francisco: Collins Liturgical, 1986), p. 292.

Week 9

Mother Teresa, *Words to Love by. . .* (Notre Dame: Ave Maria, 1983), p. 75.

Week 10

Madame Jeanne Guyon, *Experiencing the Depth of Jesus Christ* (Goleta, CA: Christian Books, 1975), pp. 75–76.

Week 11

Jean-Pierre de Caussade, *The Sacrament of the Present Moment*, trans. Kitty Muggeridge (San Francisco: Harper & Row, 1982), p. 79.

Week 12

Hannah Whitall Smith, *The Christian's Secret of a Happy Life* (Westwood, NJ: Fleming H. Revell, 1952), pp. 93–94.

Week 13

Tom Sine, *Wild Hope* (Dallas, TX: Word, 1991), pp. 1–2.

Celebrating Meditation

Thomas Merton, *Contemplative Prayer* (Garden City, NY: Doubleday, 1971), p. 89.

Hans Urs von Balthasar, *Prayer* (San Francisco: Ignatius Press, 1986), pp. 130–31.

Madame Jeanne Guyon, *Experiencing the Depth of Jesus Christ* (Goleta, CA: Christian Books, 1975), p. 4.

Brother Lawrence, *The Practice of the Presence of God* (Philadelphia: Judson, n.d.), p. 26.

Celebrating Prayer

Karl Barth, *Evangelical Theology: An Introduction* (New York: Holt, Rinehart and Winston, 1963), p. 160.

Sue Monk Kidd, *God's Joyful Surprise: Finding Yourself Loved* (San Francisco: Harper & Row, 1987), pp. 209–10.

Donald G. Bloesch, *The Struggle of Prayer* (San Francisco: Harper & Row, 1980), p. 72.

Frank Laubach, *Learning the Vocabulary of God: A Spiritual Diary* (Nashville: The Upper Room, 1956), p. 20.

Celebrating Fasting

Tito Colliander, *Way of the Ascetics: The Ancient Tradition of Discipline and Inner Growth*, trans. Katharine Ferré (San Francisco: Harper & Row, 1960), pp. 76–77.

Arthur Wallis, *God's Chosen Fast* (Fort Washington, PA: Christian Literature Crusade, 1986), p. 41.

Richard J. Foster, *Freedom of Simplicity* (San Francisco: Harper & Row, 1981), p. 138.

John Wesley, *The Works of John Wesley*, ed. Albert C. Outler, vol. 1 (Nashville: Abingdon Press, 1984), p. 60.

Celebrating Study

C. S. Lewis, *Mere Christianity* (New York: Macmillan, 1952), p. 75.

Karl Barth, *Evangelical Theology: An Introduction* (New York: Hold, Rinehart and Winston, 1963), p. 171.

Elizabeth O'Connor, *Search for Silence* (Waco, TX: Word, 1972), p. 119.

D. Elton Trueblood, *The New Man for Our Time* (New York: Harper & Row, 1970), p. 125.

Celebrating Simplicity

Walter Rauschenbusch, "Prayers of the Social Awakening," in *Voices from the Heart: Four Centuries of American Piety*, ed. Roger Lundin and Mark A. Noll (Grand Rapids: Eerdmans, 1987), p. 239.

A. W. Tozer, *The Pursuit of God* (Harrisburg, PA: Christian Publications, 1948), p. 27.

Vernard Eller, *The Simple Life* (Grand Rapids, MI: Eerdmans, 1973), p. 70.

Arthur G. Gish, *Beyond the Rat Race* (New Canaan, CT: Keats, 1973), p. 173.

Celebrating Solitude

Søren Kierkegaard, *Purity of the Heart Is to Will One Thing*, trans. Douglas V. Steere (New York: Harper Torchbooks, 1956), p. 197.

Andrew Murray, *Abide in Christ* (Springdale, PA: Whitaker House, 1979), pp. 121–22.

Catherine de Hueck Doherty, *Poustinia: Christian Spirituality of the East for Western Man* (Notre Dame: Ave Maria, 1975), p. 21–22.

Mother Angelica, *Living Prayer* (Ann Arbor, MI: Servant Books, 1985), p. 91.

Celebrating Submission

Gretchen Gaebelein Hull, *Equal to Serve* (Old Tappan, NJ: Revell, 1987), p. 200.

Thomas à Kempis, *The Imitation of Christ*, trans. William C. Creasy (Macon, GA: Mercer University Press, 1989), p. 96.

Marie Anne Majeski, *Women Models of Liberation* (Kansas City, MO: Sheed & Ward, 1988), p. 45.

Gilbert Bilezikian, *Beyond Sex Roles* (Grand Rapids, MI: Baker, 1985), p. 164.

Celebrating Service

Donald B. Kraybill, *The Upside-Down Kingdom* (Scottdale, PA: Herald Press, 1978), p. 280.

Karl Barth, *Evangelical Theology: An Introduction* (New York: Holt, Reinhart and Winston, 1963), p. 184.

D. Elton Trueblood, *The New Man for Our Time* (New York: Harper & Row, 1970), pp. 81–82.

Gretchen Gaebelein Hull, *Equal to Serve* (Old Tappan, NJ: Revell, 1987), p. 239.

Celebrating Confession

Paul Tournier, *Guilt and Grace* (San Francisco: Harper & Row, 1962), pp. 172–73.

Thomas à Kempis, *The Imitation of Christ*, trans. William C. Creasy (Macon, GA: Mercer University Press, 1989), p. 116.

Helmut Thielicke, *Our Heavenly Father: Sermons on the Lord's Prayer*, trans. John W. Doberstein (New York: Harper & Brothers, 1960), p. 104.

Jeffrey Sobosan, *Act of Contrition: Personal Responsibility and Sin* (Notre Dame: Ave Maria, 1979), p. 11.

Celebrating Worship

C. S. Lewis, *Letters to an American Lady*, ed. Clyde Kilby (Grand Rapids, MI: Eerdmans, 1967), pp. 35–36.

Robert Barclay, *Barclay's Apology in Modern English*, ed. Dean Freiday (Manasquan, NJ: Dean Freiday, 1967), p. 254.

Stephen Crisp in *Christian Faith and Practice in the Experience of the Society of Friends* (Richmond, IN: Friends United Press, 1960), p. 246.

François Fénelon, *Christian Perfection* (Minneapolis: Bethany, 1975), pp. 135–36.

Celebrating Guidance

Dallas Willard, *In Search of Guidance: Developing a Conversational Relationship with God* (Ventura, CA: Ragal, 1984), p. 33.

George Fox, *The Journal of George Fox* (Cambridge: Cambridge University Press, 1952), p. 11.

John Baillie, *A Diary of Private Prayer* (New York: Macmillan, 1977), p. 21.

Saint Augustine, *The Confessions of Saint Augustine*, trans. E. M. Blaiklock (Nashville: Thomas Nelson Publishers, 1983), p. 15.

Celebrating Celebration

Dag Hammarskjöld, *Markings*, trans. Leif Sjoberg and W. H. Auden (New York: Alfred A. Knopf, 1964), p. 56.

Hannah Whitall Smith, *The Christian's Secret of a Happy Life* (Westwood, NJ: Fleming H. Revell, 1952), p. 228.

Joan Chittister, *Wisdom Distilled from the Daily: Living the Rule of St. Benedict Today* (San Francisco: Harper & Row, 1990), pp. 108–9.

Calvin Miller, *The Legend of the Brotherstone: The Wise Men's Search* (San Francisco: Harper & Row, 1985), p. 83.